D0843655

Dedication

It takes a man with a great deal of self-assurance to be able to really support his wife's career—especially when it is inconvenient.

This book is dedicated to that man.

Preface

Our greatest joys, deepest sorrows, most persistent problems, and devastating disappointments all come from our relationships with other people.

From early childhood, we long for that absolute closeness with others—that kind of free-flowing acceptance, approval, rapport, and respect that we imagine exists in the "perfect family." Of course, most of us never really find it, or if we do find it, it doesn't last for long. Our parents, siblings, and other relatives turn out to be only human, as do the partners we fall in love with and those whom we adore as idols, leaders, colleagues, and friends. There seems to be something "missing" in our relationships. We are often left wondering if it's even possible for two people to be truly happy with and understand each other.

The answer is yes and no. We probably will never be able to achieve 100 percent rapport with another individual, at least not on a sustainable basis. That's because people are incredibly complex and in a constant state of change. Considering how little most of us understand ourselves, how could we ever hope to comprehend the mysteries of others? On the other hand, if you look around, you will find those individuals who seem to have a natural knack for getting along with others. They seem to hold a special place in our hearts, and we trust them instinctively because there is something very special about the way they connect with us. These are the people we gravitate toward and choose for long-term relationships—they spark a feeling of belonging in us.

Anyone can become one of these socially adept people—even you! And that is what this book is all about. It all begins with knowing and understanding yourself. The better each of us understands ourselves and our unique behavior characteristics, the less "baggage" we will bring to our relationships with others. This personal growth gives us a well-defined starting point from which to enhance the possibilities in any relationship. We start from knowing our strengths and do not depend on others to give us our sense of identity.

This book explains the different behavior types and the characteristics of each—how each person is a unique combination of traits and influences that serve as predictors for behavior and decision-making styles. In other words, an individual's traits can be measured, and this measurement can then be used to determine the ways the individual prefers to relate to other people. This information will help you understand why some people prefer to spend time alone while others love to be surrounded by people, why some people want to talk all the time while others prefer less frequent verbal interactions, and why some people always want to be the leader while others are content to follow. With this information, you can look at relationships from a perspective of understanding how the behaviors might, or might not, fit.

This book will also teach you how to apply this understanding to your current or past relationships at home, at work, and in the community. Suddenly, you will see why one person is offended by the things you say or do while another seems pleased by your behavior. You will see more clearly how you are viewed by people with behavioral traits that differ from yours and why particular individuals are drawn to you. You will learn how to predict potential pitfalls in relationships based on the "chemistry" that typically occurs between certain styles.

Becoming skilled at relationships is one of the most important things you will learn in life. It has the potential to transform your daily existence, bringing you more happiness in your personal life and relationships than you could imagine and enabling you to succeed in your career beyond your wildest expectations. In a significant, yet less direct way, it will also bring joy to those people around you, those you come in contact with, because your happiness and success will cause a ripple effect that travels throughout humankind.

So open these pages and embark on an exciting journey into yourself and into the hearts and hopes of those around you!

Marti Eicholz, 1998
Kirkland, Washington

Acknowledgments

Many people were involved, both directly and indirectly, in the preparation of this book. Mothers and daughters, fathers and sons, husbands and wives, brothers and sisters, friends, companions, partners, sweethearts, children, teenagers, business people, and seniors all shared their stories of self-awareness and relationships during the course of my research in behavior analysis.

The real-life dramas of all who contributed form the basis for the insights I gained during this work, and their experiences shine as a beacon of hope and inspiration to others. For their courage, generosity, and trust, I wish to thank them all.

Special Recognition

to

Alesa Lightbourne, Ph.D.
Collaborator and Contributor.

CREDITS:

Editor: Cathie Dayton
GrammarWorks: Cherie Tucker
Typesetting: Donna Baxter
Cover Design: Michelle Bartanen
Production: Kathleen Smith

All material in this publication is protected by copyright.

Copyright © 1998 by Dr. Marti Eicholz. Cover Images © 1998 PhotoDisc, Inc. All rights reserved.

No part of this written material may be copied or reproduced in any form. This written material is protected by and all rights are reserved under the copyright laws, conventions, and treaties of the United States of America and other countries.

Library of Congress Catalog Card Number 97-090824   ISBN 0-9653100-3-5

First Printing March 1998.

Personal Relationships

*The Art of
Living Together*

MARTI EICHOLZ, Ph.D.

Contents

Part Three: Becoming Aware of Each Other

Part Four: Understanding Your SAS Results

Part Five: The Chemistry of Interpersonal Relationships

Part Six: Communicating

Part Seven: Sharing Yourselves With Each Other

Part Eight: Appreciating and Supporting

Part Nine: Healing Relationships

Part Ten: Creating Fulfillment

Part Eleven: Appendix

How to Use This Book

This book is about knowing yourself, knowing your partner, and understanding how to relate to each other. It is your discovery of who you are, how you adjust to your environment, how you perceive your partner, and how your partner perceives you. It will help the two of you identify your style of communication, how you take charge, and what motivates you.

This book goes beyond the conventional discussion of relationships. You are not expected to simply read and consider this information. Instead, *Personal Relationships—The Art of Living Together* encourages you to *experience* yourself and a partner, close friend, or family member in a new way, by fully using your imagination, intuition, feelings, and the facts provided by your Self-Awareness Survey (SAS) results.

In each part, you'll find stimulating and thought-provoking questions and activities. These serve to draw out what you may already know about yourself and your partner, to teach you about the behavior styles, and give you knowledge to enhance your relationship.

Because *Personal Relationships—The Art of Living Together* is organized to help you move to progressively deeper levels of understanding yourself and others, you may want to read the parts in order. However, feel free to follow a sequence that fits your own individual style. Jot down your ideas in the margins and highlight passages that are particularly relevant to you. Regardless of the path you choose, the important thing is that when you have finished, this will truly be *your* book.

Although there is no right or wrong way to use this book, here are some suggestions that may make it easier for you to learn and remember the new material:

- For the most accurate results, it is a good idea for you and your partner to have completed the SAS before reading Parts Four and Five. This way, the information you learn will not unconsciously affect your survey responses.

- After graphing your SAS results, privately read Parts Four and Five with your results in hand.

- After reading Parts Four and Five alone, read Parts Five and Six with your Partner. This should generate a lot of questions. Rejoice, for the journey has only begun.

- Continue to read and explore the rest of the parts, always thinking about how they apply to you. Discuss the impact of the information on you, how you relate to it, and what you want to do with it.

- You will gain even deeper insights when you work through the book a second or third time.

- Some of the material contained in this book may trigger ideas, memories, and feelings. When this happens, jot down thoughts as they occur to you. These experiences can provide additional insights into your concerns or thoughts and help you define goals.

- Look for patterns or themes in your highlighting and margin notes. Where you see a pattern, you may discover a hidden strength, growth point, or an unresolved issue.

- Take your time. Enjoy your experience. Every day is an opportunity to discover something new about yourself and your friends.

As you read, highlight points that stand out to you so you can easily review them.

Part 1:

*Learning the Flow
of Relationships*

Introduction

Relationships are the spice of life. Some you are thrown into, while others you choose. However they develop, relationships are an inescapable part of life. As John Donne penned so eloquently, "No man is an island." From the moment of birth, our lives consist of starting, developing, and ending relationships. Throughout our lives, we are attached to others by a variety of "lifelines," where we alternate supporting and leading others to ensure a better life for ourselves and a better life for others—our family, friends, neighbors, work associates, life partners, children, and even generations to come.

Because relationships are so much a part of life, it stands to reason that being "good at" relationships should be considered an important skill, one that is taught to us in our early years, and one that we continue to focus on as we grow. Sadly, this is often not the case.

For most people, learning about relationships is a haphazard, trial-and-error process. We usually try very hard to make our relationships succeed—at least in the beginning. But if they fail, we often don't know why. We start again with new people, but the relationship ends up the same—because we didn't understand what went wrong in the earlier relationship. Or perhaps you have been one of the lucky ones and have a wonderful relationship with someone. But when that person grows and changes, or you do, will you know how to keep the relationship strong?

Once in a relationship, you face the reality that the other is different—yes, *really* different. At times, it is as if they are from one planet while you are from another. Differences often draw people together, but over time those same differences may tend to push those same people apart. It is important to understand that different does not mean "deficient" or "less valuable." Often we look at our partner and make judgments about the differences we see, judgments which can become barriers us. That need not continue.

This book uses the words *friend*, *other*, and *partner* in a generic way, intending to capture the breadth of your relationships. Also, in accordance with the most recent (and generally accepted) style guides, both masculine and feminine singular pronouns are referred to with the plural (and not gender-sensitive) "they."

In every relationship, some things work while others do not. A high degree of compatibility means that more things work than do not. People in relationships with a high degree of compatibility expend less energy on keeping the relationship together than those with less compatibility. Depth in a relationship occurs when there is a high degree of compatibility, though high compatibility does not presuppose a happy relationship. It does suggest that the relationship has a better chance of successfully facing issues because of an abundance of resources.

Where does compatibility start? It starts with self-knowledge and self-appreciation, because the common denominator in every relationship you have with others is that it is based on the relationship you have with yourself. At the heart of most relationship difficulties is an unresolved issue from previous relationships. Often, the problems you face have more to do with yourself than with the other person. With this knowledge, you can build better relationships by learning how to relate better to yourself. To the extent that you know, like, and even love yourself, you can love, like, or at least coexist with others. Every effort made to both understand and appreciate yourself is like well-invested money. It grows until you can rest in its abundance and live contentedly.

The TV Celebrity Meets His Match

Daniel is one of those people who gets noticed wherever he goes.

A former linebacker for a professional football team, he now hosts a TV sports commentary show that is broadcast in six states. He wears handmade suits from the city's most expensive tailor, drives a late-model Porsche convertible, and is on a first-name basis with the governor. His expansive waterfront home is the setting for gala events that frequently make the newspaper's society page.

Daniel's natural behavior makes him enjoy life in the limelight. He feels happiest when surrounded by other people, and needs ongoing social approval to feel good about himself. At the same time, he needs to feel that he is in control of most situations, which he achieves by exuding charm and warmth. People often are amazed afterward by his ability to persuade them that his idea was really in their own self-interest.

4

PART ONE: LEARNING THE FLOW OF RELATIONSHIPS

Fortunately for Daniel, his current sports commentary show lets him be his own boss to a large extent. No one ever has to tell him when to take charge. When he isn't given a leadership position, he takes one. This talent hasn't served him as well in the past, such as when he tried being an assistant coach at the state college. A couple of power struggles with the head coach, and he was out on his ear. He had similar problems trying to fit into the corporate world, where he chafed so much at the paperwork required of a sales representative that he ended up quitting in disgust.

As the host of his own show, however, Daniel is clearly in his element. He lavishes his assistants with compliments so everyone at the TV station vies to work with him. He knows how to draw out the best in the athletes he interviews, almost as if he has an invisible connection with their minds and hearts, and can therefore ask just the right questions to make them shine. The odd thing is that he can make himself shine at the same time, so everyone comes out looking like a winner.

But sometimes he is pulled in different directions—between the need to be loved and the need to be the boss. Nowhere is this more evident than in his relationship with his 15-year-old daughter, Rachelle, during the stormy years of her adolescence. This is due, in part, to the fact that Rachelle has almost exactly the same behavior styles as her father, and she can be just as flamboyant and headstrong as he can.

Rachelle lives for ballet and she is already known as the best ballerina her age in the state. Talent scouts have approached her about attending one of the world's most prestigious ballet schools in London. The offer is clearly the chance of a lifetime. It would involve a fully paid scholarship, but Rachelle would have to drop out of high school for the time being and finish her studies with a tutor during off-hours. There are not many off-hours for girls destined to be stars. She doesn't care. She dreams about going to London day and night.

DRAFT 2/5/98

Daniel, violently opposed to the idea, has forbidden Rachelle to even consider leaving home until she is 18 and graduates from high school. Sometimes he wonders whether his resistance is due to the fact that Rachelle will be so far away from him. Even imagining her inevitable departure from home several years from now, he doubts he will be able to bear the agony of missing her. Being so much alike, she is even more important to him as a companion and soul-mate than his wife.

On the other hand, sometimes he thinks that Rachelle is right and he's just being stubborn. Would he have liked the London idea better if he had come up with it himself?

Whether the roots of their struggle lie more in father and daughter's similar behavior styles or not, the fact is that Daniel and Rachelle have reached an impasse. The mere mention of the words "dance," "school," and "ballet" are enough to set one or the other off into a rage. This is unfortunate because a decision must be made very soon about the London school's offer. And in the meantime, neither Rachelle nor her father is getting their needs met for mutual affection.

The fights at home have become unbearable. Father and daughter hurl insults and threats at each other night after night. The next morning Daniel is emotionally wrung out, grateful that somehow he restrained himself from hitting her, but deeply ashamed nevertheless at how the situation has gotten out of control.

By understanding the innate strengths and struggles that come from their interpersonal chemistry, Daniel would find an answer to his current dilemma. He would understand that people with his make-up need to develop more tolerance and learn to genuinely respect the wishes and viewpoints of others. Whether or not Rachelle ends up moving to London is really not the issue. It is much more important that both of them heal their relationship so that wherever she lives they will have a deep and meaningful rapport.

Since people with Daniel's behavioral characteristics tend to dominate conversations, he should practice his listening skills—not at all the same as his interviewing skills, which are designed for audience appeal. Instead, he must place his undivided attention on Rachelle and mirror her responses with "active" listening techniques that validate her emotions and nurture trust.

In doing so, he will discover a deeper picture of her motivations. He may find, for instance, that there are other factors pushing Rachelle toward London—perhaps an unpleasant rivalry at school, a desire to see new places, or even the current discord with her dad.

When Daniel models more patient behavior and listens as a loving, concerned parent, Rachelle will sooner or later begin to follow his example and will notice immediate benefits in all her relationships. The other students will stop viewing her as a prima donna and will include her in more activities. She will avoid the loneliness that star billing often brings. Instead, she will learn that a wise tempering of extremes creates a well-rounded and satisfying life.

Become active listeners so each feels valued. Maintain the connection.

Fred, the Retiree

Fred is a 63-year-old engineer who retired just eight months ago from his lifelong job with an aircraft manufacturer. Although he had looked forward to his retirement for years, talking about all of the projects he planned to begin and hobbies he intended to pursue, instead he has sunk into a deep, disturbing depression. The energy he normally felt upon waking up in the morning has vanished, and he has a hard time even getting out of bed. Worst of all, he feels confused about "who he is"—a sure sign of self-esteem issues. His wife, Roslyn, urges him to see a counselor.

Fred finds it difficult to open up with the counselor; he asserts that everything is just fine, that he's just feeling a little blue, and his mood problems will pass. In an effort to highlight specific details, the counselor suggests examining Fred's behavioral traits through a profiling tool. Based on the results, she is able to ask Fred the types of questions that will help him look at his situation more realistically.

As it turns out, Fred was a supervisor at the aircraft company, in charge of an entire department of hourly workers as well as a number of junior- and mid-level engineers. He was accustomed to overseeing their work on a regular basis, making decisions that were considered essential by his own superiors and "taking charge" of his workgroup whenever leadership was required.

At home in retirement, however, it's just Fred and Roslyn together all day long. Roslyn has established a comfortable routine during her decades as a homemaker and has her own way of doing things. When Fred tries to display "leadership" or take command of the household routine, Roslyn gets irritated. Rather than being appreciative, she seems almost resentful of his presence in the house.

Fred is therefore trying to do his best to conform to what Roslyn wants. He bites his tongue when a decision is called for and allows his wife to carry on as she always has. Often, this causes Fred a great deal of turmoil, as he can see that his input could make things run more efficiently and often more cost-effectively. Why won't she re-use the perfectly good (and free) plastic grocery bags to line the trash can, for instance, instead of purchasing bags the exact size from the store? Why does she insist on buying expensive cleansers for the kitchen countertops when economical baking soda would do just as well?

He is making similar attempts to dampen his natural outgoing, exuberant, talkative behavior. Roslyn is a quiet soul who enjoys reading by the fire, sewing in her corner off the dining room, and walking the dog alone every afternoon. Fred, on the other hand, wants constant companionship. So he follows Roslyn from room to room, "entertaining" her with bits of information he has gleaned from the morning newspaper, recounting stories from his days in the workforce, and asking her for praise on his various projects. Rather than responding positively, as he expects, she has become downright crabby and sullen, avoiding him whenever possible, and shutting herself in the guest bedroom for inordinately long periods of time.

Fred is trying to be more tolerant and easygoing. His attempt could be viewed as a noble move in character development away from his natural impatience. But the effort comes at a price, as Fred's bottomed-out satisfaction and energy scores indicate.

The counselor asks Fred to explain why he feels the way he does. They discuss his energy, which is worrisomely low, in the range where one normally experiences frequent accidents, prolonged illness, substance abuse, or serious psychological problems. His general satisfaction is so low that it's almost off the chart. Although the counselor cannot come right out and say so, she knows that Fred's self-esteem must be practically nonexistent at this point—because he is expending so much energy on being someone he is not.

Viewing his data, Fred has graphic evidence of the magnitude of his self-esteem issues. In particular, he must come to terms with the fact that his Dominance is not being channeled effectively, as he has little opportunity to practice leadership. This begs the obvious question: does he like the accommodation he is currently forcing on his behavior, or would he rather be doing something else with that energy?

Fred decides that he needs a more creative outlet. There is little hope of Roslyn's changing the patterns she has developed over the past 30 years, nor is there any likelihood that she will become more appreciative of his influence or constant presence.

So Fred enrolls in an executive volunteer program, which takes him out of the house three days a week. As part of the program, he acts as an unpaid consultant to start-up engineering firms, helping them with both technical and management elements. This has proven to be an important self-esteem booster for Fred, as the young engineers are grateful for his seasoned perspective, and they listen as intently as his employees used to when he gave orders at the aircraft company.

The volunteer program also gives Fred the social interaction he needs; he meets new people every day and is beginning to build a sizable network of contacts within the community. As a result, he is less reliant on Roslyn's company when he comes home and is more willing to let her have uninterrupted spells of quiet time.

In a few months, when Fred has adjusted to his new volunteer position, he will probably want to do another behavioral profile as a follow-up. This will allow him to measure progress toward his goals and quantify the fact that his self-esteem is, indeed, improving.

Sarah and Kelly—Conflict as an Opportunity for Growth

Imagine two friends who are engaged in conflict over their differences. Sarah and Kelly have been friends for years. Their relationship is built around an appreciation of the arts. Although they do not talk to each other daily, it is rare for more than two weeks to pass without them getting together to attend a concert, go to a gallery showing, or simply to take in a movie together. While they share an interest in cultural activities, their behavioral styles are very different. Kelly makes decisions quickly and intuitively, while Sarah muses over Kelly's request for a day or two before agreeing to participate.

Sarah often reminds Kelly of her own father, who took "forever" to make a decision. When she was a teenager, he took so long deciding if Kelly could go to the "Sadie Hawkins" dance that by the time he said yes, the boy she wanted to ask out had already accepted another invitation. Like Sarah, Kelly's father was also more of a follower than an initiator—invariably, his answer to "What would you like to do today?" was "I don't know. What do you want to do?" Kelly always suspected that her father ended up agreeing to do things he didn't really want to do.

Sarah's experience is quite different. As the youngest child tagging along with her older brothers and sister, Sarah was often told "Go away! We don't want you here!" So, as she grew up and started developing her own friends, she thrived on being asked to join others. And though she almost always ends up saying yes to invitations, she likes to take time to savor the pleasure of having been invited. Also, Sarah is uncomfortable with uncertainty and doesn't like making mistakes, so her natural inclination is to take time to decide. That way, she can be sure that she won't have to change her mind later.

PART ONE: LEARNING THE FLOW OF RELATIONSHIPS

Although Kelly doesn't mind being the instigator of their activities, she worries that perhaps she is being too pushy and that she should let Sarah take the lead occasionally. So, when a singer they both like scheduled a performance in their city, she decided to let Sarah be the one to suggest that they attend. As the concert date approached, Kelly assumed that Sarah must be very busy because she never called to talk to Kelly about the concert. Meanwhile, Sarah, who was waiting for Kelly to call to invite her to the performance, felt discouraged and rejected because Kelly hadn't called.

In the end, Kelly went to the concert by herself, regretting that her friend wasn't there with her, but believing they still have a strong relationship and that they will probably catch another event together soon. Meanwhile, Sarah sat at home, dejected, both because she missed the performance and because she believes that her friendship with Kelly is ending.

A few weeks after the concert, Sarah and Kelly ran into each other at the mall and Kelly mentioned how much she enjoyed the concert. From Sarah's reaction, Kelly could tell her friend was upset, but she couldn't understand why. After all, if Sarah had wanted to go to the concert, all she would have had to do was ask. As for Sarah, she was hurt by what she perceived as Kelly's rejection and insensitivity—first by not inviting her and then by "rubbing it in" with talk of how much fun the concert was.

The friends part both frustrated and puzzled by the other's behavior. While on the surface, their conflict was over a concert invitation, in reality, their conflict is over the differences in their natural behavioral styles. Sarah takes time to think before committing herself while Kelly leaps ahead and, if needed, changes her mind and leaps another direction. Sarah and Kelly are almost opposite when it comes to their natural style. Sarah's way of satisfying her need for inclusion is at war with Kelly's way of overcoming her history with her father. Kelly does not "see" Sarah but sees her father. Kelly wants to change her history by changing Sarah, but Sarah cannot imagine initiating an engagement. After all, her need for inclusion is what motivates her. Kelly's learned behavior is in conflict with Sarah's natural self.

Sarah is naturally a thinker and goes with the flow, while Kelly is naturally energetic and full of ideas. Kelly likes to *have* a following while Sarah likes to follow. As long as Kelly appreciates *her* natural self, that of a leader, and Sarah honors her natural self, they get along. When Kelly wants Sarah to change, Kelly is not appreciating her own natural self and in return does not appreciate Sarah's natural self either.

This case study illustrates how differences can affect relationships. In this example, instead of treating this situation as a minor squabble over a concert, or a major fight about rejection and laziness, Sarah and Kelly can save their friendship, and, in fact, even strengthen it. Although it might be easiest to ignore the problem—either by pretending it wasn't important or by ending the friendship—the best approach for these women is to treat this conflict as an opportunity for growth and discuss their differences to come to an understanding of the other's natural self.

The only reason that any conflict can't be immediately settled is that one side is holding on to an irrational position for energy purposes.

Circular Life of Relationships

Building a strong, healthy relationship with another person can be thought of as a circle that begins, oddly enough, with *becoming aware of the self*. It requires that we pay attention to our deepest selves and learn what our inherent strengths and weaknesses are. Then we will realize what each of us has to offer a friend or partner. We begin to notice how we typically interact with others so we can evaluate our actions and consider how we could become more sensitive and caring. With this growing self-awareness come opportunities to move to deeper levels of intimacy in our relationships.

Observe yourself.

Next, we nurture our *soul, mind, body, and spirit* to solidify the inner growth that occurred during our introspective period. This nourishes our sense of self, of who we are, and integrates all the parts of our being.

Nurture your soul, mind, body and spirit.

Now we are at a place where we are ready to *share our "self"* with another person openly and with a sense of excitement about the possibilities for harmony. Our prior inner work makes us more likely not to repeat communication mistakes that we made in past relationships. Being in this place with our "self," we are more likely to express ourselves more genuinely and therefore attract potential relationship partners who are themselves at this same state in their life's evolution.

Share yourself.

Observe and listen to others.

During this sharing of self, we also *observe and listen* carefully to the other person in the relationship. We participate in an easy giving and taking of information, noticing all the while how our comments are received by the other person through body language, tone of response, and ability to validate verbal messages we are sending. We also notice how we receive the information the other person is sending, using these same gauges.

Over time, we assimilate our observations and build a foundation of *understanding*. We learn about the other person's attitudes and habits so we can eventually predict his or her behavior fairly accurately. Through mutual respect, we support the other person's *individual discoveries and unique aspirations,* and that person does the same with us. Thus, the two in the relationship grow closer together and create rapport—harmony, meaning, and fulfillment. In short, this is a true relationship, one likely to withstand the test of time because the partners feel safe to express their innermost selves.

Understand, support, and accept others.

The following graphic illustrates this circular life of relationships.

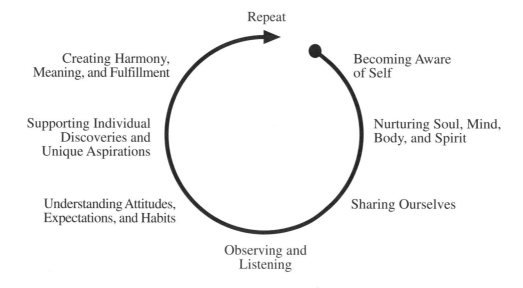

Self-nurturing is a flame. Once we have a flame, we can pass it on and light other people's torches. This flame, this strength and courage, comes from deep inside each of us and becomes our gift to ourselves and to others.

It takes hard work to maintain a relationship. The key is having a desire to learn about yourself and a willingness to communicate clearly.

Part 2:

How Relationships Develop

PART TWO: HOW RELATIONSHIPS DEVELOP

Introduction

With rare exceptions, we are all involved in relationship of different kinds—relationships with parents, siblings, husbands, wives, partners, team members, co-workers, and others. Consider for a moment all the individuals in your life with whom you are partners in a relationship. When two or more individuals come together in a relationship, there is a "connection"—a natural mode of relating. You associate with these individuals to deepen that "connection"—combining individual talents to create a whole greater than any of the parts alone. In the beginning, the "connection" is usually warm, accepting, understanding, and allows for errors.

In any relationship, you have a wonderful opportunity to build something new. The "connection" is a unique system between two or more individuals who meld and modify their individual needs to act and make decisions through the relationship. The interaction between you and your partner, or you and the group, is unique, and because of this relationship, new thinking, new actions, and new possibilities occur. The process of building the "connection" often requires a great repertoire of skills to support the needs of others. In this part, you will learn how relationships develop and progress, and you will be able to understand how you and others interact on a daily basis.

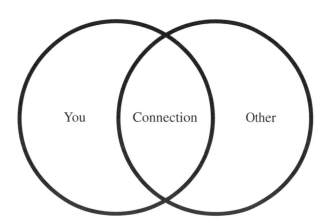

"The meeting of two personalities is like the contact of two chemical substances: if there is any reaction, both are transformed."

– Carl Jung

Starting

Starting a new relationship includes gaining new information about yourself and your impact on the other person. New relationships are exciting—every word shared is golden. Possibilities abound and hopes flourish. You are overwhelmed with expectancy and hang onto the other person's every word and gesture. Below the surface, however, the two of you are observing and gathering information. Based on this input, you reach one of two conclusions—to continue the relationship or to end it. In a personal relationship, you may reach such an agreement in a matter of moments.

Many times throughout any healthy and growing relationship, you and your partner will begin again or reconstruct your agreements by gathering new information. Often, these new agreements mean that you need to forgive past behavior or give up unfulfilled expectations. You may have to adjust your expectations to be more in line with the reality of the relationship and its history.

When we continue to gather information about our relationships, they grow and become stronger. It is common for partners to stop gathering data once a relationship is formed. But it is the continued gathering of information and sharing of truths about experiences in the relationship that allow—and promote—the growth of each partner and the relationship itself.

Don't be fooled by thinking that it is easier to relate on the basis of assumptions rather than on the truth. You may *think* it's easier to continue relating to another person the way you have always done, rather than trying something different. But be forewarned: this type of behavior can be the road to disaster.

Insanity is doing the same thing over and over and expecting different results!

Over time, it is possible for you to create fresh mental images about your partner.

Think about it:

- What assumptions or beliefs do you have of the other in your life? (Example: She's an unsafe driver. He jumps to conclusions.)

- Check these assumptions against your partner's current behavior to see if they are true now or were ever true.

- Watch and listen for comfort level. You may notice that a behavior means something other than what you intended. You may wish to seek additional information. Ask questions and learn from the interaction.

- Avoid assuming. It is easy to assume that others want to be treated just as you would like. Your assumptions about another's needs, expectations, or behaviors are often incorrect.

- Express yourself at a deeper level and encourage your partner to do the same—get in touch with your feelings. If relationships are based on maintaining the status quo, they lack life and vitality. Create new and wonderful experiences in the relationship through gaining additional information. Give an extra hug. Express a concern you would have otherwise left unsaid. Discover the rich possibilities when you experiment with new behavior.

If you adopt this behavior, you will discover new treasures in your current relationships. After all, it was the newness of information that originally attracted you to this particular person, so work to uncover the volumes of undiscovered information within each existing partnership. This new information is sure to challenge you. Consider what you will do with it. Where does it fit into the relationship? How will you relate to it?

> "'Mental Models' or mental images are deeply ingrained assumptions, generalizations, or even pictures or images that influence how we understand the world and how we take action."
> – Peter Senge

> Don't be like the mother who forces her little boy to put on his jacket whenever *she* feels chilly.

> Keep relationships fresh by constantly looking for new facets—in yourself and in your partner.

Wrestling

New information creates a *wrestling* within and between partners. A type of competitiveness arises, as you and your partner try to silently negotiate a power structure. *Wrestling*, the second stage of a relationship, is perhaps the most difficult time.

A relationship's developmental stages are dynamic, meaning you will constantly be gaining information, wrestling, ruling, and working at some level.

Wrestling occurs in every relationship. The goal at this stage is to learn about yourself and gain a sense of equality. This sense of self and feeling of equality will become the hallmark of this particular relationship.

When *wrestling* occurs, and it surely will occur, your task is simple—learn about yourself. Many tools are available; the SAS, included in this book, is one of them. Another tool presented in the book *Straight Talk* by Miller, Wackman, Nunally, and Saline, is the "awareness wheel."[1] The wheel consists of five elements: sensations, interpretations, feelings, intentions, and actions.

Sensations refer to any stimulus: sound, sight, touch, taste, or smell. Sensations communicate your world to you. Interpretations are the mental images and words that you experience from these sensations; these include your set of rules and beliefs about the sensations. Sensations, and your interpretations of them, often stimulate emotions. Your emotions, in turn, create an intention to take action or cause something to happen. Actions are the behaviors you do because of your interpretations.

Doing what you have done in the past is easier than doing something different. To do something new takes forethought and effort.

---

[1] Miller, Wackman, Nunally, and Saline, *Straight Talk*, (Penquin Books, New York, 1982).

Can you see how these elements affect your behavior in relationships? When you interact with others, you may be able to guess what stimulates a particular behavior in them. Try matching their actions to the words they use to explain their beliefs and rules about a situation. For example, have you ever been in a situation where a friend is angry at you? Yet the friend smiles while saying "I'm really mad at you for breaking your commitment to me last night." Smiling probably isn't the action you would expect from someone who is mad. Often times, partners exclude important elements from conversations that make their actions incongruent with the words being spoken. These may include:

- Facial expressions or words that don't match emotions
- Unshared thoughts and rules about emotions
- Unexpressed wants for yourself, others, and the relationship
- A lack of disclosure about past, present, and proposed future actions

In short, there's more *not* being communicated than is. Try using the elements of the "awareness wheel" to improve or broaden your skill at meaningful communications.[2] This tool can help you create the rules that will build a relationship in which you can communicate your truths clearly while each of you—and the relationship—evolves.

All real living is meeting.
– Martin Buber

---

[2] Ibid. 4

Ruling

This leads us to the third stage of how relationships develop: *Ruling*. *Ruling* is building a living system together. Both partners need to take time to co-create rules about how they will relate to each other and to the outside world. These rules are important because they will govern the relationship. When you share your rules with each other, you create a mutual vision about how you will get and keep what you want in the relationship. "We always arrive fashionably late." "I mess up the kitchen, and you clean it up." "You take care of the money, and I'll take care of the kids." These are examples of the countless agreements, made either consciously or unconsciously, as a relationship progresses through the *ruling* stage. Think of these "rules" as mental place holders for the processes that guarantee certain results. They are meant to provide each partner with a measure of control in the relationship. And this control ensures some degree of safety.

Each person has different rules based on their deepest beliefs. You might be wondering, "What exactly are *my* rules?" To answer that, let's look at some more examples. Are you superstitious? Do you knock on wood after talking about good fortune? Superstitions are an extreme form of beliefs and their rules. When a specific event occurs that triggers a superstitious rule, it causes you to behave in a certain way. Chances are if you believe you are in for seven years of bad luck when you break a mirror, you will attribute all the bad luck you have for the next seven years to breaking the mirror.

Much of the *wrestling* that takes place in relationship is about whose rules will be the ones obeyed within the relationship. Remember, each rule is about a process and therefore guarantees some result or action. What do your rules guarantee? Is something missing for you? Do you and your partner have conflicting rules, or do they promise the same results? Can either of you get your desired results by changing your rules to match the other person's? And, when you change your rules, do you change your behavior?

Lester likes a cozy home, well-lit and warm at all times. Lucy believes it's important to conserve energy, so she's always turning off lights and lowering the thermostat. They will need to negotiate a "rule" about the heat and electricity before they can live together happily.

When Carl was a boy, his father made all the decisions in the family. In Pam's home, however, it was her mother who ruled the roost. Carl and Pam clearly have very different ideas about the "right" way to run a household. During the *ruling* stage of their relationship, this will be a very important point to resolve, so they can move on to create a relationship that *works*.

You and your partner can invent a new set of rules that grow out of your differences. You can agree to a compromise. Or, there may be times when you and your partner let both your rules, or your ways of doing things, co-exist. This is known as appreciating your differences.

Working

Once you have an acceptable process in place for *ruling*, the relationship naturally moves to the next stage, which is called *working*.

Working is a stage of collaborative and harmonious living. Collaborative efforts require time, energy, trust, and emotional exposure. Only after you have laid the foundation and established the rules to resolve issues in a relationship will you and your partner be able to find the time and energy, and have enough trust in one another, to work on living together.

This is the point in your relationship where you find harmony in your life together. You form a pattern where the behavior of one partner suggests the response of the other partner—you become like a single instrument playing the song of life. Partners achieve a level of togetherness that is interdependent based on harmonious independence. The actions of one partner do not dictate the behavior of the other (but may suggest it). Then, according to the joint rules, both partners act in such a way that is best for the relationship. Partners realize that they are living not solely for the *self* but for him- or her*self* in the relationship. At this point, you will have graduated to a level of interdependent living that is based on a harmonious balance of independence and inter-dependence. The key is to remember and learn from all that you have gone through to get to this point (illustrated in the following figure).

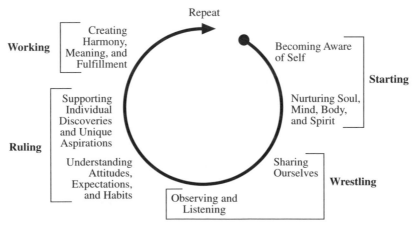

What's Next?

As you move into Part Three, you and your friend have an opportunity to take the Self-Awareness Survey (SAS). Once the two of you chart your results, you'll be able to better understand your natural selves and gain insight into the natural self of the other. You will learn more about why you behave and interact the way you do. It will clarify what is unique about you, and you will learn specific strategies for communicating more effectively with your friends, partner, and other family members.

It can also be useful to validate the information from your SAS by having a close friend or companion fill out a survey as to how you are perceived. Together, this information can help you get to the root of conflicts you may be experiencing in personal relationships because the information helps you understand how you're coming across to others. As you increase awareness and cultivate an understanding and appreciation of others' differences, you can then use these differences to help your relationships grow.

Self-awareness allows new information into your relationships.

Part 3:

*Becoming Aware
of Each Other*

PART THREE: BECOMING AWARE OF EACH OTHER

Introduction

Are you ready to see yourself in a new light? Would you like to become conscious of yourself and others in your life in a completely new way? This part will give you a framework to enhance your self-awareness. With this awareness, you will be able to improve both your personal life and your relationships.

Relationships do not take care of themselves. They require thoughtful maintenance and a commitment to understanding the person(s) you are in a relationship with. Truly understanding another person means being open to discovering things about that person that may be difficult to accept.

This journey to become aware of each other is not as difficult as you might think, but it does require the courage to face—and the willingness to accept—whatever you find when you look. The journey is full of surprises and not all of them are pleasant. You may discover qualities about each other and your ways of relating that you wish were different. In Part Four you will learn ways to change those things, but you can only make such changes after you understand and accept *YOU* today.

And both of you will discover that you already have everything you need to create the rich and rewarding life you want and deserve.

> **We have to dare to be ourselves, however, frightening or strange that self may prove to be.**
>
> – May Sarton

Behavioral Traits and Energy Level

First, we will explore the four primary behavioral traits. They are Dominance, Extroversion, Patience, and Structure. Characteristics of these traits are discussed below:

- **Dominance**—The Dominance (D) behavioral trait is the "control/drive" trait. Individuals who have a high Dominance factor tend to act on their environment, controlling their environment through their actions and directives.

- **Extroversion**—The Extroversion (E) behavioral trait is the "social/relations" and "people/fluency" trait. Individuals who have a high Extroversion factor also tend to act on their environment. But they tend to control their environment through people.

- **Patience**—The Patience (P) behavioral trait is the "rate of motion/adaptable" trait. People who have a high Patience factor are usually in harmony with, as well as influenced by, their environment and proceed through life at a steady, comfortable, cautious pace.

- **Structure**—The Structure (S) behavioral trait is the "systems-oriented/quality assurance" trait. People who have a high Structure factor tend to be keenly aware of and sensitive to their environment and traditions.

**Dominance: our
need for control
and results.**

**Extroversion: our
sociability.**

**Patience: our
sense of timing.**

**Structure: our
need for order.**

As you learn about the characteristics of these four behavioral traits, you will begin to view other people differently. It's best, however, to begin by learning about your own traits first. Then team this understanding with the ability to recognize characteristics of others' behavior, and you will be able to communicate and work with others more effectively.

Individuals have a unique combination of traits that influences their attitudes and actions.

In addition to the four primary behavioral traits, there is an additional element of behavior that should be considered when discussing a person's characteristics, namely energy.

- **Energy level** refers to the amount of energy you have to complete a task, your physical and mental energy, as well as your motivation. Your available energy is influenced by heredity, as well as by any illnesses or other stressors (positive or negative) in your life.

Each person possesses a certain amount of each of these behavioral traits. The strength of the trait (its presence or absence) determines a great deal about people's behavior: how they relate to others, whether they are outgoing or shy, how well they tolerate rules, and whether they are impulsive or tire easily.

None of the behavioral traits are either good or bad in and of themselves. There are no "ideal" behaviors, so be open minded. By understanding what your primary behavioral traits are, you'll learn which tools to use when considering aspects of your personal relationships. You'll be able to assess whether certain roles or relationships will be a good "match" for you, which ones will promote your personal development, and which will inhibit your growth.

Be open minded. There are no "ideal" behaviors.

Additional copies of the survey (SAS) are available in the appendix.

PART THREE: BECOMING AWARE OF EACH OTHER

To begin the journey of understanding yourself and each other, take the Self-Awareness Survey (SAS). When you discover your partner's unique combination of traits, you will begin to understand why he or she acts in a certain way, and you will learn more effective ways to interact to achieve greater satisfaction in the relationship.

You can take SAS and score it yourself using the instructions in this book. You can also take it online and have a computer-run report prepared. The report is produced using very sophisticated software, with techniques that have been validated on millions of people around the world. To learn more, visit the SAS web site at www.transforming.org.

Another way to understand more about each other in the relationship is to review Part Three and work through the exercises. You and your partner will gain insight into yourselves, and if each of you is willing to share that information with the other, you will gain valuable new information about each other that can enhance the relationship.

You will learn what each of these word groups means in Part Four. But please don't read ahead. It's essential that you make your word group choices before doing a self-analysis of your behavior.

The SAS presented on the following pages is designed to help you map your behavioral traits. You will each use the information from the SAS to construct a graph that illustrates your behaviors and energy level. Individually, select words or phrases from specific word groups, then use these selections to construct a graphical representation of your own behavioral profile.

The SAS worksheets contain seven groups of words or phrases for each of the four behavioral traits (Dominance, Extroversion, Patience, and Structure) and energy level. For each of the categories, select the word group that best describes you. Make your selection quickly and spontaneously, without giving a second thought to your choice. Trust that your inner self will know right away which group "fits" best. These choices describe your internal descriptions, those characteristics that are true of what you are thinking or feeling inside, but which may not be obvious to other people. Identifying these primary behavioral traits will help you understand your thoughts and actions.

In working through this activity, try not to focus too heavily on any individual word or on whether each adjective in the set fits you totally. The objective is to determine where you fall along a continuum. Select only one box for each of the categories (e.g., one for D, another for E, and so on).

Although these word groups, and the behaviors they represent, are discussed in detail later in the book, it is important not to read ahead before you make your selections.

Trust your inner self. Make your selections quickly and spontaneously. Try not to focus too heavily on any individual word or adjective.

Your Self-Awareness Survey

1. Select the word group that best describes you:

D1	D2	D3	D4
· placid · subservient · lacking in self-confidence · yielding · submissive · fearful · easily taken advantage of · never assertive · extremely gentle	· meek · genuine · dependent · hesitant · deferring · submitting · apprehensive · selfless · rarely assertive · very gentle	· mild · gentle · peace-loving · modest · composed · sometimes assertive · congenial · willing · humble · soft · yielding	· certain · curious · discreet · supportive · sometimes leader · sometimes follower · adaptable in groups · relatively assertive

D5	D6	D7	Write selection:
			(For example, D2)
· firm · competitive · decisive · confident · self-assured · definite · positive · happy as leader · usually assertive	· forceful · aspiring · authoritative · bold · direct · adventuresome · keen · analytical · the leader, or nothing	· cynical · brazen · superior · aggressive · commanding · fearless · daring · sharp · courageous · always assertive · criticized for cruelty	

2. Select the word group that best describes you:

E1	E2	E3	E4
· withdrawn · secretive · socially selective · aloof · solitary · loner · skeptical · crowd-hater · lost in inner world	· individualistic · shy · serious · introspective · pensive · confidential · timid · guarded · uncomfortable in crowds · happy in solitude	· contemplative · reserved · quiet · private · creative · imaginative · selective · communicative · enjoyer of inner-world · thoughtful	· poised · neighborly · sincere · earnest · genial · friendly · sometimes alone · sometimes social · flexible with others · comfortable as both star and wallflower

E5	E6	E7	Write selection:
			(For example, E4)
· fun-loving · enthusiastic · friendly · humorous · cordial · optimistic · good-natured · convincing · group-oriented · often center of attention	· eager · light-hearted · joyful · hospitable · fluent · trusting · exciting · decisive · innovative · rarely alone · almost always in group · usually center of attention	· promoting · talkative · gregarious · zealous · effusive· demonstrative · lavish · eloquent · never alone · always center of attention · very public person	

3. Select the word group that best describes you:

P1	P2	P3	P4
· brusque · impetuous · coiled spring · sporadic · intense · short-focused · volatile · out of control of emotions · always impulsive	· quick-witted · swift · innovative · driving · hasty · abrupt · reactive · impatient · urgent · often impulsive · prioritizer of own agenda	· active · quick · fast-paced · restless · initiator · action-oriented · pusher · pace-setter · on occasion impulsive	· easy-going · adaptable · adjustable · responsive · sometimes long fuse sometimes short fuse · balanced agenda with others

P5	P6	P7	Write selection:
			(For example, P4)
· patient · dependable · accommodating · steady · thoughtful · amiable · mild · non-judgmental · non-demonstrative · occasionally angry	· compassionate · cooperative · consistent · kind · sensitive · warm · persistent · emotion avoider · altruistic · rarely angry	· stoic · selfless · hider of emotions · unhurried · passive · hesitant · tolerant · sympathetic · complacent · saint-like patience · never angry · indifferent	

4. Select the word group that best describes you:

S1	S2	S3	S4
· antagonistic · hostile · disagreeable · resistant · defiant · self-governing · disobedient · rebellious · anti-establishment · iconoclast	· disliker of authority · resentful of orders · free-thinker · adventurous · contrary · disavower of rules · very independent · visionary	· multi-faceted · "big picture" type · unstructured · uninhibited · broad-minded · rational-izer · not fond of details	· supportive · orderly · open-minded · curious · sometimes compliant · sometimes rule breaker · adaptable · obstreperous · tolerant of many perspectives

S5	S6	S7	Write selection:
			(For example, S4)
· procedural · faithful · systems-oriented · detailer · dutiful · steadfast · committed · careful · fussy about details · relatively obedient · well-orga-nized · enjoyer of structure	· disciplined · methodical · highly obedient · conscientious · devoted · concerned · cautious · fond of details · often fearful · perfectionistic	· subservient · live by the book · exacting · meticulous · dependent · stickler for *all* rules · over-preparer · super-perfectionist · sometimes paralyzed by fear	

5. To determine how much energy you have to accomplish tasks, select the word **G** group that best describes your present state. It is important to note that your response may vary according to your current life's circumstances. For the purposes of determining your present energy level, select how you have felt most frequently during the past month or two:

G1	G2	G3	G4
· accident-prone · often sick · a substance abuser · lethargic · seriously depressed · suicidal · surrounded by life crises	· easily fatigued · unfocused · difficulty completing projects · overwhelmed · inactive · illness prone	· sufficient energy · sometimes ill · limited exercise · average productivity · easily diverted	· moderate energy · productive even with diversions · average health · normal fitness · sense of well-being

G5	G6	G7	Write selection:
			(For example, G4)
· plenty of energy · strong · healthy · rarely exhausted · enjoyer of exercise · productive all day · resilient	· endless energy · competent to handle myriad projects at once · hard driver · in need of lots of stimulus · frequent exerciser	· extraordinary energy · overpowering · tireless · dynamo · never ill · never still · constantly restless	

Complete Your Graphs

Using the results of your word-group selections, complete your personal profile on the blank graph on the following page. Note that the first bar is labeled D. Use your selections from the Group 1 (D) boxes to shade in the appropriate number of spaces (e.g., D1, shade in one space, D2, shade in two spaces). Shade in the appropriate spaces for each of your other selections (i.e., Group 2 [E], Group 3 [P], Group 4 [S], and Group 5 [G]).

This graphing system is completely arbitrary. Low bars do not denote deficiencies in any way. The graph could just as easily be turned upside down with the white spaces represented at the bottom. In fact, during our discussions, these white or blank boxes will be used to assess the "flip" side of each of the behavioral attributes.

Unfortunately, it is characteristic for humans to be all too eager to see their faults rather than acknowledge their strengths. It is therefore important for you, particularly at this point in your self-awareness, not to jump to any conclusions that might alter the self-awareness possibilities inherent in this analysis tool or in your relationship.

Your Self-Awareness Graph

Name: _____   Date: _____

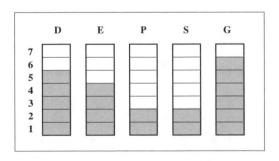

	D	E	P	S	G
7					
6					
5					
4					
3					
2					
1					

D = Dominance   E = Extroversion   P = Patience   S = Structure   G = Energy Level

Sample Graph

A Brief Look at Your SAS Results

As you look at your personal behavioral graph, determine which is your highest trait—the trait with the most boxes filled in. This trait is your predominant behavioral descriptor, which will affect 50 to 85 percent of your behavior. Sometimes people will have two traits of equal strength. When this is the case, both traits exert equal influence in predicting how you will react in different circumstances.

How many of your behavioral traits score above 4? These are your "high" traits. Most people have two high traits and two low traits. A small percentage of individuals will score high in only one behavioral trait. When this is the case, these are called "pure" traits, influencing about 85 percent of the individual's behavior.

An individual may score high in three traits. It is very rare, nearly impossible, for an individual to score high in all four traits.

Which of your traits are relatively low, scoring in the range of 1 to 3? These traits are very important to understanding who you are. Don't think of them negatively. Remember, low doesn't mean deficient.

A score of 4 in a particular area means that you are highly adaptable in that area and can adjust your behavior as circumstances require. If you have only one score of 4, and most of your other scores are higher or lower, the 4 may be extremely significant in that it reflects an adaptability in that area to fluctuate high or low. In other words, your behavior is unpredictable. See Example 2.

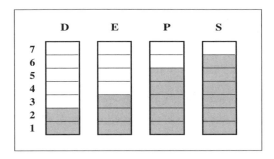

Example 1:
This person is high in Structure and Patience.

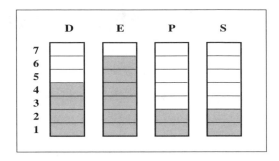

Example 2:
This person is a "pure" Extrovert—only a single high trait.

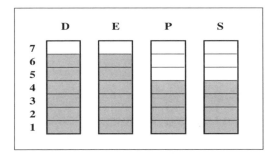

Example 3:
This person is high in Dominance and Extroversion and flexible and adaptable in Patience and Structure—the P and S scores fall at the mid-point range.

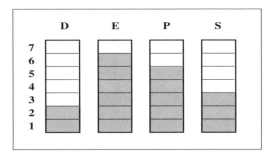

Example 4:
This person is high in Extroversion and Patience and low in Structure and Dominance.

Verifying Your Self-Assessment Survey

Before we describe the characteristics of each behavioral type, let's verify that your survey scores are accurate and make sure that you placed yourself where you feel most comfortable on the behavioral graph. The following exercise will confirm your graph results so you can avoid any confusion that could result from your interpretation of certain words within the word groups (because certain words can have different meanings to different people).

From the boxes on the following pages, select either the top (high) or bottom (low) box as the one that "feels" most like you.

High D

THINGS I WANT:	THINGS I LIKE:	THINGS I DON'T LIKE:
challenge	risk-taking	details
power	being in charge	vagueness
money	delegating to others	mediocrity
material things	responsibility	indecisiveness
prestige	challenge	laziness
authority	direct answers	small talk
position	bottom-line results	shy people

Low D

THINGS I WANT:	THINGS I LIKE:	THINGS I DON'T LIKE:
protection	harmony	discord
peace	stability	forcefulness
clear direction	security	gambling
predictability	strong leaders	criticism
fairness	tolerance	conflict
mutual respect	going with the flow	making lots of decisions
		egotistical people

How would you describe yourself? _____ High D _____ Low D _____ Somewhere in between

High E

THINGS I WANT:	THINGS I LIKE:	THINGS I DON'T LIKE:
status	talking	pessimists
popularity	having an audience	loneliness
money	brainstorming	technical challenges
praise	surprises	criticism
public recognition	parties	isolation
be part of a group	playfulness	being bored
flamboyance	sense of opportunity	egotistical people

Low E

THINGS I WANT:	THINGS I LIKE:	THINGS I DON'T LIKE:
respect	intimate settings	exhibitionists
ideas	a few close friends	practicing in public
opportunity to be creative	good planning	speaking before groups
time to think	peace and quiet	politicking
privacy	discretion	ad-libbing
	thoughtfulness	insensitive people

How would you describe yourself? _____ High E _____ Low E _____ Somewhere in between

High P

THINGS I WANT:	THINGS I LIKE:	THINGS I DON'T LIKE:
harmony	being helpful	pressure
justice	predictability	poor planning
cooperation	stability	intolerance
routines	going with the flow	selfishness
leisure time	fairness	pushiness
consistent pace	sense of calm	conflict

Low P

THINGS I WANT:	THINGS I LIKE:	THINGS I DON'T LIKE:
excitement	action	time on hands
more time in the day	change	being bored
new situations	surprises	delays
travel	life in fast lane	inflexible routine
stimulating environment	impulse decisions	deliberation
quick gratification		

How would you describe yourself? _____ High P _____ Low P _____ Somewhere in between

High S

THINGS I WANT:	THINGS I LIKE:	THINGS I DON'T LIKE:
accuracy	respect for rules	risks
quality	sincerity	clutter
clear directives	security	flattery
validation	pre-planning	big talkers
sense of structure	order	fickleness
	formality	rule changes
	consistency	

Low S

THINGS I WANT:	THINGS I LIKE:	THINGS I DON'T LIKE:
independence	thinking "outside the box"	paperwork
unusual assignments	casual environment	authority figures
personal freedom	delegating to others	regulations
adventure	making own decisions	feeling "boxed in"
	exploring	the mundane
		rigidity

How would you describe yourself? _____ High S _____ Low S _____ Somewhere in between

Review your choices from the preceding pages and prioritize your answers at the bottom of each page. Look at each of the traits you identified as high. Which one of these traits "feels" like it describes you the best? Write that trait as your *Predominant Trait* on the following list. Write your second strongest trait next to *Secondary Trait*. Rank the next two and write the answers next to *Tertiary Trait* and *Least Important Trait* below.

	Your Traits	Your Partner's Traits
Predominant Trait:	_____	_____

Identify your highest trait or traits if you have two with the same intensity.

Secondary Trait:	_____	_____

Identify your second-highest trait.

Tertiary Trait:	_____	_____

Identify your third-highest trait.

Least-Important Trait:	_____	_____

Identify your lowest trait.

You will end up with something	like this:	or this:
Predominant Trait:	E	D
Secondary Trait:	P	S
Tertiary Trait:	S	P
Least-Important Trait:	D	E

This ranking should match the information on your behavioral graph. If it does not, adjust your behavioral graph as needed.

Your Energy Level

The energy level refers to the amount of energy you have to do a task, as well as your vigor and enthusiasm. Think of your energy level as the capacity and charge of your "battery." Unlike a battery, however, your energy level can vary greatly depending on the stress and environmental pressure you are experiencing.

The most observable and hereditary behavioral factor is our energy level. It is only affected by energy drain (including past issues and health issues) or adrenal pump.

We are all energy fields. Scientists tell us that waves of energy are constantly flowing out from us and into us whether we are aware of it or not. Your essence is this energy. Everyone in close range can detect these energy patterns, thus our feelings of attraction and repulsion. For example, you can probably notice energy changes, both positive and negative, in group dynamics. In some gatherings you feel invigorated. Others make you feel restless, irritable, or fearful. How are you using the energy within you, and how are you transmitting that energy into the world around you?

Review your individual self-awareness graph and answer the following questions about your energy level.

When you're free to do what you love to do, you don't fatigue as easily.

Exercise 3-1: Assessing Energy

Assessing Your Energy

Check one:

What is your energy level?
___ High   ___ Medium   ___ Low

How would you describe your energy level?

___ Higher than I would like

___ About right for me

___ Lower than I would like

How do you use your energy?

___ Very high efficiency

___ About average efficiency

___ Tend to waste my energy

Assessing Your Partner's Energy

Check one:

What is his/her energy level?
___ High   ___ Medium   ___ Low

How would you describe his/her energy level?

___ Higher than I would like

___ About right for me

___ Lower than I would like

How does he/she use his/her energy?

___ Very high efficiency

___ About average efficiency

___ Tend to waste my energy

Energy Level in Relationships

What does it mean if you have a different energy level than the people you find yourself in relationships with? Should you dump your current girlfriend because she's a live wire and you're a couch potato. Should you drag your teenage son out of bed whenever he tries to sleep until noon?

As with any other behavioral trait, there is no "correct" match between people when it comes to energy level. We can all think of countless examples of successful marriages or partnerships where two people have nearly identical energy levels—and an equal number of successes where energy levels are widely divergent. The answer lies in defining the kind of relationship you want and being clear about what you expect from the significant people in your life.

You are unique in a world of energy. You can consciously project your energy.

Michael is the vice president of sales and marketing for a global electronics company. He jets around the world on a continual basis, stopping home for a weekend or a week or two, and then heading off to high-powered meetings and conferences in Buenos Aires, Delhi, Tokyo, and Paris. He loves a fast-paced lifestyle, enjoying the constant stimulation and adrenaline rush of a career-on-the-go. He prides himself on never being sick, jogging six miles a day no matter where he finds himself, and getting by on as little as four hours of sleep a day. Obviously, he scores very high on the energy scale.

Michael's wife, Jennie, is just the opposite. Even during high school she was known as a home-body, happy reading a book or doing needlepoint in favor of more strenuous activities. She's worked part-time in the office of an elementary school for many years, and feels comfortable with a slow but steady routine. If she doesn't get eight hours of sleep a night, she feels positively ill the next day. She has had problems with depression off and on over the years but her doctor has been unable to determine whether it might be due to thyroid difficulties, hormone levels, or simply the stress of running a family virtually alone whenever Michael is out of town.

Could we say that the marriage is a success, energy-wise? To Michael it is, because he is getting all of his needs met. He has a perfect outlet for his extraordinary energy; yet he also has a back-up person keeping the family together for him. When he breezes into town, he hits the house like a tornado, filling it to bursting with his vim and vigor. There are days filled with hikes and ball games with his two sons and late nights of intimacy with Jennie. He crams a month's worth of fathering and husbanding into 48 hours. Then he's off again—and Jennie refills the refrigerator and cookie jar, washes mountains of laundry, pays all of the bills, and generally settles back into a slower, less demanding routine.

The question of a successful marriage looks somewhat different from Jennie's perspective, as we must wonder why she suffers from chronic depression. Of course, it's possible to have a lower energy level and still be perfectly content with your life. This tends to be the case as people age; they come to grips with their reduced energy reserves and stop feeling guilty about taking naps. This inner reconciliation also often occurs when people are recovering from an illness or are on strong medication; they understand the reason for their fatigue or lethargy, and accept it as inevitable until they are back to normal.

But given Jennie's depression, it's unlikely that she is completely happy with her life as it stands today, and she needs to ask herself some difficult questions to get to the bottom of her discontent. Does she feel somehow inferior to Michael because of his non-stop energy? Does she belittle herself for not living at his fast pace? Perhaps he makes jokes when she lies down for a rest or when she won't join him on a run around the neighborhood. Or maybe she resents his long absences and the extra work it creates for her holding down the fort alone.

Before their marriage, Michael dated many women whose energy level matched or even exceeded his own. He found these relationships oddly unsettling; while they sizzled briefly, they fizzled just as quickly. It became clear to him that he needed a partner with a steadier pace—and even though he suspected that Jennie might seem boring to him as the years wore on, he was willing to sacrifice some of the excitement of a tireless traveling mate for the emotional security that Jennie offered.

Jennie had also dated men more like herself in energy quotient and had almost married a clerk in the local post office. She deliberately selected Michael instead, however, feeling that he represented an opportunity for greater personal growth than the postal worker. She knew it was unlikely that Michael would change much to accommodate her. If anyone adapted to the energy level difference, it would have to be her. But this was a change she felt willing to make, sensing that the marriage would open new horizons for her.

Now the rubber is hitting the road when it comes to Jennie's inner adjustments. And adjustments, especially behavioral ones, are not always easy to make. So Jennie finds herself resenting Michael's rushed schedule and his requests that she stay up later than she would like for sex. She braces herself before he returns home each time, knowing that she'll have to summon up energy that is hard for her to find. She begrudges him, in fact, the very "push" that she knew (and hoped) would occur in a lifetime with a man like Michael.

Entire books have been written on the subject of energy level: how to get more energy, refine your energy, change its direction, develop more peaceful energy, and so forth. Our purpose here is to simply observe energy differences as they affect relationships, so that partners will have a meaningful tool for articulating these differences and making decisions about future directions.

In the case of Michael and Jennie, for instance, both partners might decide to compromise. Michael could try to tone down his activity level while he's at home, and Jennie could try to rev up her energy thermostat. Or they might decide that only one of them should change (it could be either one, depending on how they want the relationship to evolve). They also might decide that the energy issue is an irreconcilable one, and neither partner wants to change enough to salvage the marriage. In this, as in all relationship questions, it's totally up to the individuals involved.

There are pros and cons to being at either end of the energy spectrum, and it's often a challenge to understand the viewpoint of people who are currently at the opposite end. High energy people often think that theirs is the only tempo that makes sense, and they see other people as sluggish, lazy, and maddeningly slow. "What's wrong with the rest of the world that they can't keep up with me?" they think. Low energy people, on the other hand, can feel intimidated by individuals with more horsepower, whom they consider to be hyperactive and unpleasantly intense. "What's the big hurry?" they wonder. "Why can't these fast-track people take it easy and rest every now and again?"

Many times, outside forces or even chemical conditions affect our energy level. High energy people might be clinically diagnosable as hyperactive or having attention-deficit disorder. They may habitually use stimulants, like excessive amounts of caffeine, nicotine, or non-prescriptive drugs. Or they may just be extraordinary healthy, and blessed with seemingly endless mental, physical or emotional reserves. Often highly gifted children need much less sleep than others their age, for example, as do people who get frequent strenuous exercise.

Low energy can be attributable to many factors as well. Sometimes it is indicative of poor health, mental turmoil, or other disturbing conditions that act as a "drag" on a person's normal energy reserves. People with low energy can be accident-prone or unusually susceptible to illness. They may suffer from seasonal affect disorder (SAD) or light deprivation symptoms from living in a dark or dreary climate. Others become lethargic due to living in an extremely hot or humid area. Sometimes low energy is caused by substance abuse or by prescription drugs. Or when we go through highly stressful times, such as a death in the family, divorce, move, or job termination, our energy reserves typically plummet.

But despite these environmental and physical factors, it's also essential to remember that a large part of our energy quotient is determined by genetics. As any mother with more than one child can tell you, each baby exhibits its own unique energy style from birth. One kicks and moves around a lot, walks early, and sleeps little. Another takes long naps, is in no big hurry to walk, and plays contentedly for hours in its playpen. This is why we shouldn't be critical of our own (or our partner's) energy patterns. None of us is in total control of the amount of energy available to us at any given time.

When you consider your energy, and compare it with your partner's, be careful not to be judgmental. Neither style is "best" or "right." Instead, assess whether your styles are compatible right now, given what each of you want from the relationship. Examine whether either low or high energy quotients might be a cause for medical or psychological concern. If not, discuss how content each of you is with the way things are and whether you feel the need for behavioral changes—or increased mutual understanding.

The Importance of Your Highest Trait

You now know what your predominant behavioral trait is: Dominance, Extroversion, Patience, or Structure. And you have your individual self-awareness graph (how you tend to see yourself). Review your high traits from these materials, remembering that your highest trait influences 50 to 85 percent of your behavior.

Now consider the magnitude of your highest trait. The distance of your trait from the midpoint (4) on the graph indicates the degree to which this trait affects your feelings, thoughts, motivations, and actions. For instance, if your highest trait is Dominance, your natural style could range from being a self-assured organizer to someone who has a sense of superiority and can be quite demanding.

Each trait column represents a continuum, with intensity building the farther you go on either side of the midpoint. If a trait registers at the midpoint, its influence will be mild. If all of your behavioral traits fall at the midpoint (4), you are likely to be a very flexible and easygoing person.

If you have one or more traits that register close to the top of your graph, it is likely that you experience life intensely.

Simply put, behavioral traits can be within these ranges:

- Dominance can range from demanding to dependent, with emotional extremes from cruelty to acceptance.
- Extroversion can range from talkative to thoughtful, with extremes being very public or private individuals.
- Patience can range from easygoing to emotional, with extremes from indifferent to urgent.
- Structure can range from structured to independent, with extremes of obedience or rebellion.

Keep in mind as you review these materials that your highest trait, as well as the intensity of your traits, should not be construed as positive or negative. Your SAS graph is not an indicator of "good" or "bad." It is not a measurement of worth. It is simply information for you to use on your journey of self-awareness.

Perhaps one of the most useful things you will take away from this book is new insight into some of the underlying subtleties of human interactions and what you personally bring to those interactions. For some, it may be disconcerting to discover that they act differently than they thought they did or than they would like. They may feel their survey is telling them they are dishonest. In actuality, nearly all of us make some concessions in order to get by in our lives—compromises that divert us from our inner, authentic selves. Your survey results and the information in this book are designed to provide you with the means to identify the adjustments you are making and what they cost in terms of your overall satisfaction with life.

Are you really expressing the person you were born to be?

By developing a clearer understanding of your inner strengths, you may also discover that some of the adjustments you are making are simply unnecessary. Perhaps doing what you truly want to do, in a way you truly want to do it, will get you the results you desire because you will be performing at your highest level.

Take charge of your life and decide which labor pains you are willing to experience in order to give birth to yourself.

PART THREE: BECOMING AWARE OF EACH OTHER

Part 4:

*Understanding
Your SAS Results*

Introduction

Just as the SAS will help you understand your behavioral characteristics, it will also help you better understand anyone you are in a relationship with—and help you appreciate your differences.

Always remember that *this information should never be demanded from your partner*. It is a worthwhile learning and growth experience, and it will enhance the relationship, only *if you have the other's consent*. Also remember that your objective as a loving partner should be to support your partner in becoming the person he or she truly *wants* to be (as opposed to the person you think he or she should be). And, you can help your partner achieve greater personal satisfaction only if you have a clear understanding of his or her inner strengths.

Understanding the Four Behavioral Traits

To give you some perspective on how relationships can be affected by the combination of different traits, let's review some recent case studies. See if you identify with any of the individuals in the case studies or if they remind you of someone you are in a relationship with.

The Dominance Behavioral Trait

What do you think when you hear that someone is a "dominant" person? You might say that person is "controlling," "aggressive," or even "powerful." And you'd be right. As a behavioral trait,

The wise approach for effectiveness and success is to learn your own style and then adapt to the other styles around you.

however, Dominance is much more than just these descriptors. A person with high Dominance is also innovative, persistent, and often a brilliant problem-solver.

Most of us think we can recognize others who exhibit dominant behaviors. The dictatorial boss, the domineering politician, and the recalcitrant teen may all be examples of people who display high Dominance. But people may not always be who we think they are. In fact, they may be the opposite. The following example illustrates why.

Meet Darcy and Jim

Darcy met Jim when she was an editor at a large publishing house in New York. Jim was a senior designer, and the two dated for a year before they married. They were both in their 30s at the time and had concentrated on developing their careers rather than on relationships in their 20s.

Darcy was known for keeping her authors on a short leash and for winning most arguments about story content. With a fiery personality, she considered herself to be assertive, strong-willed, and, at times, even "controlling." When she met Jim, she was impressed by his creativity and his easygoing nature. He seemed to be the perfect fit for her as a life mate. Darcy decided early on that, most of the time, she could call the shots in her marriage, just as she did at work.

It took Darcy a while to realize that although Jim appeared mild-mannered and non-demanding, he was always in control of situations, both at work and home. He often controlled others by adopting passive-aggressive behavior—waiting patiently for someone else to react. Other times, he promised to do something, and then would conveniently forget. The more Darcy pushed, the more Jim stonewalled.

You Can't Tell a Book . . .

When Darcy and Jim looked at their SAS graphs, Darcy was shocked by the results. She scored extremely low in the Dominance behavioral trait, while Jim scored high. His laid-back attitude masked a powerful personality. And although Darcy thought that she was Dominant, despite her occasional temper, she was actually more peace-loving and congenial.

What Does High Dominance Mean?

Because the Dominance trait is considered the "control/drive" trait, people high in Dominance (also called "High Ds") often get what they want—or keep trying until they do. High Ds tend to control their environment through their actions and directives. Jim, for example, would buy Darcy expensive "thinking of you" presents when he wanted to convince her to accompany him to the opera.

It is important to understand that High D people tend to exhibit many of the following characteristics. They are: adventuresome, aggressive, authoritative, blunt, competitive, decisive, demanding, direct, forceful, goal-oriented, impatient, inquisitive, persistent, powerful, results-oriented, risk-takers, and strong-willed.

Take a Look at a High D's Behavior

Don't make the mistake of caricaturing High Ds as demanding and ruthless like J.R. Ewing in the television series "*Dallas.*" High Ds can be pleasant and generous as long as they are getting results. They *do* demand and expect a great deal from others—but also from themselves. Rather than being dictators, as might be expected, High Ds support a team approach if it fits into the selected goals. However, if they are exceptionally stressed or pressured, a High D may turn into a "steam-roller" or become dictatorial to gain control.

Steve works in a manufacturing plant and is the overseer of operations. His highest behavioral trait is Dominance. As a High D, Steve tends to challenge management, respecting only those he perceives to be competent. A natural leader, Steve likes to delegate responsibility, but not authority. He has an intense need to be in control at all times, both of the events around him and of his own emotions.

Though at times intimidating, Steve enjoys getting things done. He relishes attaining the bottom-line, meeting deadlines, and getting results, traits that help him succeed at his job.

How to Relate With a High D

High Ds can be forceful, outspoken, and frank. A key to relating successfully with them is to use direct, concise messages. For example, rather than saying to a High D partner, "It would be great if we could go to a movie sometime soon," instead you might say, "I'd like to go to a movie with you Saturday evening, if you don't have other plans."

It is also important to note that the primary emotion associated with high Dominance is anger. When in a relationship with a High D, this emotion may be very close to the surface. If the High D explodes, try not to take it personally. Often, High Ds are more mad at themselves than at others or at situations. You might think of a High D as someone who has a gruff exterior, but who is really a "marshmallow" inside.

Can You be in a Relationship With a High D—and Maintain Your Sense of Self?

High D individuals are not likely to change their level of Dominance much. However, High D partners will meet—and even exceed—your expectations of the relationship if you can bring out the best in them. To do that, you need to clearly explain your expectations and be willing to negotiate one-on-one so you don't come across as threatening.

Discover Powerful Motivating Factors

Because High Ds can have strong personalities (whether overtly or covertly), living with them can be a challenge. One way to promote a healthy relationship with a High D is to discover—and use—effective motivators.

So what motivates a person with a high Dominance behavioral trait? Some motivators may be obvious, such as allowing High Ds the position of power and authority in the relationship. Grant them as much control over situations as you are comfortable with. Give the High D freedom from controls, supervision, and details. Communicate with them precisely and directly. In Darcy and Jim's case, for example, Darcy learned to make lists for Jim that cover everything from everyday chores to who's coming over for dinner next weekend. As a result, Jim felt in control because he wasn't constantly being reminded about things.

The Extroversion Behavioral Trait

How often do you come across someone who is warm, charming, witty, and can talk effortlessly? Many people wish they were more comfortable with other people one-on-one and more extroverted. People who have high Extroversion, however, are more than just outgoing and self-confident; they are also upbeat, creative, persuasive, and confident. But sometimes, a high Extroversion trait drives people to make choices that are not in their best interests. The following example illustrates why.

Getting to Know Stacey—A "Party" Person

Stacey, 26, is single and has been on her own since she finished high school. Not knowing what career path to take, and realizing that she loved children, Stacey success-fully completed nanny school. At the end of the year, the school placed her with a family that had two daughters, two and four years old.

Because she was with children all day, Stacey started craving adult companionship. Her boyfriend worked quite a bit of overtime, leaving her home alone most nights. To get the adult stimulation and attention she wanted, Stacey started going out to bars in her neighborhood. Naturally attractive and witty, Stacey quickly found that she could easily charm men.

The down side to Stacey's night life, however, was that she had difficulty getting up in the morning after a night of partying. She found herself missing the alarm one too many times and was fired from her job. Although the family truly liked the way Stacey interacted with the children, the decline in her dependability prohibited them from keeping her on.

Achieving a Workable Balance

When a girlfriend introduced Stacey to SAS, Stacey scored above average in the Dominance behavioral trait, but scored highest in Extroversion. Her report indicated that she was, perhaps, trying to be less outgoing and personable than was natural for her.

When Stacey reviewed her SAS graph, she realized that although a nanny job gave her the chance to be with children, it didn't offer her the adult companionship and attention she really needed. For someone who was at her happiest around others, Stacey had put herself in a job where, at the very most, she communicated with a four-year old about preschool topics.

After much consideration about her behavioral traits and what she might be most happy doing, Stacey enrolled in massage school and got a job in a local health club. Interacting with people all day has increased Stacey's satisfaction level to higher than ever before. She has stopped partying on weekdays, preferring to stay at the club and socialize while she works out. Her boyfriend often joins her.

What Does High Extroversion Mean?

The Extroversion trait is considered the "social/relations" and "people and fluency" trait. People who score high in Extroversion (also called "High Es") often get what they want and seem to do so with ease. High Es tend to control their environment through people. Stacey, for example, would accept dates with other men readily just to make her boyfriend jealous.

High E people tend to exhibit many of the following characteristics. They are: affable, influential, open-minded, optimistic, talkative, trusting, self-promoting, enthusiastic, generous, inspiring, personable, charming, confident, sociable, emotional, and charming.

Recognizing High Es by Their Behaviors

People with a high Extroversion trait may appear to be carefree and positive all the time. Keep in mind, though, if you are in a relationship with a High E partner, that they are also very sensitive to what others think of them and may become defensive if challenged on believability, details, or accuracy. High Es can be very adept at talking their way out of trouble, and many have an enthusiasm to talk on and on—with or without encouragement!

Bill is a pastor who has led a large congregation for the past ten years. Affable and a powerful speaker, Bill is known as a good listener and counselor. But although he appears to be extremely outgoing, the opposite is really the case. Bill's deepest desire is to take a sabbatical, get away from the people-management aspects of his job, and concentrate on renewing his own spirituality. Bill's SAS report did not surprise him—his Extroversion trait was relatively low. Bill's strongest behavioral trait is Patience, which reflects his true yearnings.

On the other hand, the church's associate pastor, Fred, was extremely high in Extroversion. After reading both his own and Fred's graphs, Bill decided to make some long-overdue changes in the church. He called a church staff meeting and assigned some of his job duties to Fred, who was pleased to have "earned" more responsibilities. Fred took over managing the senior group activities and all church-wide events. A new youth pastor was hired to work with teen programs. As a result, Bill had additional time to study Scripture and prepare his sermons. He also continued to counsel his parishioners one-on-one and discovered that once he had more energy, he enjoyed this part of his job as well.

Whatever else you have going for you, you need faith and spirituality to complete the package.

How to Communicate with a High E

High Es have a seller/persuasive communication style. Positive and optimistic, High Es enjoy talking; some like arguing and debating simply as an intellectual exercise. To get your message across to High Es, make friendly comments and compliment them on their ideas or approaches. You might say, "I hadn't thought about that solution," or "I really like hearing feedback from you." In this way, you will create an environment in which your High E partner is more willing to listen to you.

The primary emotion associated with high Extroversion is optimism. So when communicating with a High E, try to be upbeat. High Es dislike chronic complainers and people who aren't enthusiastic—they may even be demotivated by such complaints or take them personally.

Can You be in a Relationship With a High E—and Get a Word in Edgewise?

High E individuals believe that the impossible can be done. They hold incredible optimism for the future, which may not be grounded in data or facts, making the High E appear to be a visionary or a dreamer. If you are in a relationship with a High E, you'll be most successful if you support their hopes and intentions.

High Es like to be noticed and appreciated. Make sure you ask your High E partner to contribute their ideas, and then implement these ideas whenever possible. For many High Es, it's important to combine their professional and personal lives, so plan on having plenty of "shop talk" at home.

What Motivates a High E?

If you're a social person, being in a relationship with a High E can be easy. But if you are fairly reserved and don't like "small talk," you'll need to discover effective ways to motivate your High E partner toward compromise behavior.

What motivates a person with a high Extroversion behavioral trait? A High E needs to have the freedom to socialize with others often and to experience new and varied experiences. In Stacey's case, she realized that she was not fully using her natural people skills when she was a nanny.

The Patience Behavioral Trait

When you are at a checkout counter at the grocery store, how patient are you? Do you get annoyed if the person in front of you has 12 items in the "10 Items or Less" express line? Do you rush through the store, hurriedly getting items on your list, then rush out? Or do you take time, look for new food items you haven't tried before, not caring about the crowds? How does your partner respond to these types of situations?

As you might expect, people who have high Patience are calm and easygoing. They're also sincere, deliberate, friendly, understanding, and peaceful. Many are good listeners; most are good in relationships.

Dan's situation presents a good example of the Patience behavioral trait.

Dan's Story

Dan is a self-trained technical illustrator who began his career in product support at a small software company. As the company grew, Dan took over all of the design and layout for both documentation and marketing materials. The work was occasionally rigorous, such as before a trade show, but generally Dan enjoyed the slow pace. He had enough energy left over after his job to lead a men's choir group.

Quite happy with his job situation, Dan had no thoughts of leaving until a new manager, Eric, took over his department. Volatile and driven, Eric requested that Dan keep close track of his time and the graphics budget. In addition, Eric expected Dan to issue daily status reports about all marketing projects, plus take on additional projects in the company. Dan responded willingly at first, but soon lost interest in meeting Eric's constant demands.

After a frustrating six months, Eric determined that all graphics could be done by an outside graphic design firm. Dan was laid off. At his exit interview, Dan was surprised to hear Eric say that he found Dan to be passive and lazy. Dan considered himself to be just the opposite! With a generous severance package, Dan found work immediately at a new design firm in the city.

From the Frying Pan into the Fire

Dan only lasted seven months at the new job. The pace was frantic and no production procedures had been established. Dan found that he was constantly working overtime, so he no longer had time for the men's chorus. Because he was so stressed, Dan became withdrawn, and was often absent from work saying he was sick. When he was fired, Dan felt relieved.

Before jumping into another job, Dan went to a career counselor, and took the SAS survey. Learning that Patience was his highest behavioral trait, he became determined to find a career that met his need for stability, job security, and a relaxed work atmosphere.

Based on the results of SAS, Dan decided to start his own design business at home. His first client was the software company he had left previously. With an in-depth knowledge of the company's products and with low overhead, Dan convinced his former boss that outsourcing all design work to him would benefit both of them. Eric and Dan are very pleased with the new arrangement.

What Does High Patience Mean?

The Patience behavioral trait is considered the "rate of motion" trait. People who score high in Patience (also called "High Ps") often proceed through life at a well-regulated pace. High Ps tend to be influenced *by* their environment (as opposed to Ds and Es, who act *on* their environment). Dan, for example, was much happier when he worked for a less driven manager than Eric and did not do well at all in the demanding environment of the graphics firm.

High P people tend to exhibit many of the following characteristics. They are: amiable, systematic, relaxed, mild, deliberate, understanding, non-demonstrative and steady. Many react calmly when under pressure—but only outwardly, because they do not like to cause trouble or make waves. Instead, they tend to bury their emotions deep within and process feelings in a "time-release" mode.

Can You Recognize a High P?

Many High Ps are not easy to spot. People who find comfort in crowds, like to work in teams, or join organized clubs are often High Ps (especially if they have moderate to High E traits). High Ps may look like they do not get a lot done—you may even think that they are complacent, such as Dan's bosses did. But remember the story of the tortoise and the hare in Aesop's fable. Many times, a slow, steady rate of effort can get more accomplished than a driven, erratic pace.

When Betsy married Jeff, she was impressed by how relaxed his parents seemed to be. Dinners with the in-laws were friendly, and Betsy's mother-in-law was a sympathetic listener. Because Betsy was herself extremely driven and lived her life at "warp speed," she was amazed that two people could be so easy to be with.

But soon the in-laws' behavior began to bother her. They never planned in advance and were always late to functions. When Betsy and Jeff would suggest various activities, they would decline, then suggest that everyone come to their house and play cards instead.

Betsy had taken SAS and knew that she scored low in Patience. Jeff was average in Patience, and she guessed that both her in-laws were very High Ps.

When Betsy thought about the characteristics of behavioral traits, she realized that her in-laws lived life very differently from the way she did. So, she made some immediate changes that would help her enjoy her husband's family more. First, she decided to slow down her own pace by taking up yoga. She also made sure to give her in-laws plenty of time to decide on whether or not they wanted to attend specific family functions.

Relating Successfully With a High P

Although seemingly friendly, High Ps communicate with others in a very careful, controlled manner. They often have a "wait and see" attitude, which can be difficult for others around them, especially those who do not have a lot of Patience. One way to get your message across to a High P partner is to give time to think and process what you say. Don't expect an immediate response. You might ask a High P partner, "Why don't you think about this for a few days, then let's talk again?" or "If we are going on the cruise, I need to book the reservation by tomorrow. Could you let me know by the end of today if you still want to go?"

Oddly enough, the primary emotion associated with high Patience is an apparent *lack* of emotion. A High P will avoid conflict at any cost, but may get revenge later. It's important to understand this in a relationship with High Ps. Just because they agree to something, it does not necessarily mean they like the idea. You may need to check in frequently with High Ps to ensure that they're happy with decisions.

Can You be in a Relationship With High Ps—and Ever Know What They're Feeling?

High P individuals need logical reasons for changes and often want a road map to follow. This can be a challenge in a relationship if both partners are not High Ps. High Ps need closure on issues and time to adjust to any changes. Volatile relationships are not comfortable or enjoyable for them. They like to be appreciated, not just for their efforts, but also for their loyalty.

When in a relationship with a High P, take time to clearly explain your position on issues—and don't demand immediate answers. If you show sincere interest in them and listen to them responsively, you'll find High Ps better able to commit to decisions in your timeframe. Above all, avoid threatening a High P. While it may appear that the High P has given in to what you want, you'll more than likely find you'll be left with your plans booby trapped by uncooperative behavior down the road.

How Do You Motivate the High P?

There are many effective motivators for the High P. Try these and see which ones work for you. Understand that your High P partner will probably have long-standing, treasured relationships with friends or groups of friends. In addition, give a High P partner personal attention and recognition for completed tasks. Give praise and thanks—High Ps have a great need for approval.

The High P appreciates harmonious, low-key interactions. Communicate with High Ps in a friendly, casual way. Betsy, for example, discovered that calling her mother-in-law just to chat—rather than for a specific purpose—helped create a new level of friendship between them.

The Structure Behavioral Trait

On a scale of 1 to 10, with 10 being the highest, how much of a perfectionist do you think you are? Do you consider yourself a "follower?" How detailed are you? Each of these characteristics falls under the Structure behavioral trait in the SAS. An individual with a high Structure trait is analytical, has high standards, and handles life in a systematic way.

Surprisingly, only 21 percent of the people surveyed in the U.S. have Structure as their highest behavioral trait—lower than the percentages for Dominance, Extroversion and Patience. Most of the time, we can figure out who in our social circle is high in Structure: the dedicated accountant, our immaculate friend, a conventional boss. But others may be less obvious.

Teresa and Tom—The Perfect Couple

Teresa and Tom met in high school. Teresa was a junior and Tom a senior. She first noticed him at the Junior Sock Hop, where he played in the dance band. They started dating and got married during their senior year in college.

Because Tom's first love was playing guitar and singing, he took a job in a music store during college and continued to work there after graduation. Teresa's major was business, and she was offered a job as a project assistant in her father's construction company. On weekends, Teresa watched Tom sing at local hangouts.

Eventually, Tom's band because successful enough to open for some well-known rock groups that played in the area. With a more steady income from his band's appearances, Tom was able to quit his job at the music store and concentrate full time on playing in the band and recording.

Teresa's girlfriends were jealous of her for marrying a "rock star." They always wondered how Teresa and Tom got along. Teresa, a very conservative businesswoman, spent much of her free time riding and showing horses. Tom's preference was to be involved in recording music or doing chores on their farm.

Now, Get the Real Story

Teresa and Tom completed SAS graphs early in their marriage. Teresa was worried that Tom might eventually find her too conventional, so she was more than a little surprised at the data sheet results. While Teresa scored low on Extroversion and Tom scored high, Tom's Structure trait was also very high. In fact, it was much stronger than Teresa's!

After much discussion, it turned out that Tom viewed his singing job just any other type of work, except that his job began at 9:00 p.m. on weekend nights. In truth, Tom was an exacting, reserved, analytical person who just happened to have a gift of music. Tom's high Extroversion trait made it easy for him to perform in front of crowds. His Structure trait gave him the attention to detail necessary for hours of disciplined practice. His interest in rock music, therefore, had very little to do with counterculture (or Low S) behavioral traits. As Teresa would later describe him, "He's just a typical farm boy in boots and overalls who really likes to sing."

Demonstrate pride in your partner both privately and with close friends.

What Does High Structure Mean?

The Structure trait is considered the "systems oriented/quality assurance" trait. People who score high in Structure (also called "High Ss") are keenly aware of their environment and honor traditions. They feel they have to look at everything and double-check for accuracy. Tom, for example, reviews his band's schedules and song lists daily, even if they don't change. Tom's agent has learned that this is one way that Tom feels he is in touch with—and in control of—his environment.

High S people tend to exhibit many of the following characteristics: they are exacting, have high standards, and are task-driven, conservative, courteous, perfectionistic, and systematic.

High Ss and Their Behavior

After all you've read so far about High Ss, you may think they are pretty uptight people. But that's not always the case, and their related strengths can make them very desirable as partners. For instance, High Ss are very loyal mates. They have a well-developed sense of propriety and tradition and may be the one person in your family who plans the reunions or ensures that the photo albums are kept up to date. Though formal and reserved, High Ss have a strong sense of fairness and are often judicial leaders. When under pressure, a person who has a high Structure trait may cover his or her tracks with facts or stall for time to seek more information.

Juanita has four daughters. Her youngest, Sarah, has just had a baby boy, making Juanita a grandmother for the fifth time. Juanita and Sarah do not see eye-to-eye on how to raise a baby. A High S, Juanita keeps pulling out her Doctor Spock book from the 1950s. Sarah, an action-oriented, independent sort, has a low Structure trait. Much to Juanita's dismay, Sarah keeps trying different parenting styles to see which one works best for her new son.

To Sarah, Juanita's concerns come across as judgmental and critical, even though they are not intended that way. Juanita is simply trying to do what she feels—and has learned from experience—is right.

Relating Successfully With a High S

Because High Ss are extremely conscientious, they relate to others in a guarded, cautious manner. The key to relating with High Ss is to give them clearly defined directions and present ideas in detail, correctly, and in order. Statements such as, "I'd like you to prepare the slide presentation from our trip to Mexico for dinner with the Johnstons on Friday at 8 o'clock in the evening," will help High Ss understand what is expected. In addition, assure a High S that someone is in charge, "I'll check the slides and let you know tomorrow if anything is missing. Will you have enough time to get the slides together or should we reschedule dinner?"

Note that the primary emotion associated with a high Structure behavioral trait is fear, because the High S is so afraid of being wrong. So, in a relationship with a High S, try not to make critical comments. High Ss generally dislike criticism unless you back it up with facts. In the same vein, when you praise a High S, make sure it is well-deserved.

High Ss—Easy to be in a Relationship With?

High Ss prefer to be approached with issues in a straightforward, direct way. They are most comfortable in environments where noise and interruptions are kept to a minimum. In disagreements with a High S, make sure you can prove your side with data, facts, or testimonials from respected people, and avoid raising your voice. And be sure to provide a High S partner with plenty of time to make decisions; he or she may need to research the issue or speak with someone else before making a commitment.

To strengthen the relationship with her mother, Sarah started taking Juanita to a parenting class at a local hospital. The instructor emphasized "different strokes for different folks" regarding child rearing. Sarah patiently explained to Juanita why she was trying various parenting techniques with her son. In the process, she managed to quell Juanita's fears that Sarah didn't know what she was doing. Juanita is now much more relaxed with Sarah's parenting style. In fact, she has even started changing some of her own opinions about how to raise children. The two women have enrolled in a second parenting class together.

_____

We can learn from others' experiences, but often a lesson must be brought home by the personal process.

_____

Learn What Motivates a High S

Because High Ss can be guarded, it is not always easy to know what makes them happy or to provide them with the motivators they need most.

So what motivates a person with a high Structure behavioral trait? Now that you understand more about High Ss, you may also realize that giving them facts helps to get them moving in the right direction. Another positive motivator is to ensure that High Ss get all the information they need around the issues at hand.

Once High Ss know what is expected of them, they have an incentive to accomplish things. Try not to appeal to feelings or emotions when attempting to motivate the High S, but instead provide data and facts that can help the High S make a decision. Then let the High S know when you need an answer. In Sarah and Juanita's case, Sarah left a brochure about the parenting class for her mother to read and did not pressure Juanita to attend. Juanita felt that she had complete control of her decision, which she based on facts.

Taking Another Look at Your SAS Results

With your new understanding of what your SAS reveals about you, review your graph again and consider whether you agree or disagree with any sections. Perhaps you have identified areas that you want to discuss with your partner or some other close friend.

Your SAS results outline several general descriptors and phrases that describe your natural behavior. You may or may not, however, agree with these results. Remember that you, like all of us, have some degree of each of the four behavioral traits—more or less—and a greater intensity of some than others.

Become Aware of Your "Hidden Parts"

Are you aware of any characteristic of your behavior that you might be hiding? For example: Do you always appear upbeat to others but feel irritated or down on the inside? Do you pretend to be comfortable at parties when you are really shy? Are you truly able to be yourself in your relationship?

Oftentimes, we give the impression of being comfortable when we are not because we think it is expected of us. As demonstrated by your answers to the survey you just completed, you may be presenting an image that isn't really you.

Your hidden parts are those things about you that you keep to yourself. So much, in fact, that you might not be aware of them yourself! Take a second look at any of the descriptors that surprised you. Review your answers to the survey again and see what characteristics you might be hiding. Consider characteristics unique to you and what you individually have to offer. Take a look at all your wonderful assets. Then, think about how any of your hidden parts might be keeping you from enjoying the satisfaction or success you are looking for in your relationship. Discuss what you find with your partner, who may be very interested in getting to know and understand your hidden parts.

**We often hide who
and what we really
are from others—
even from ourselves.**

Using What You Have Learned

You have been given a lot of information about how predominant behavioral traits can affect a relationship. Give yourself some time to integrate this information into your relationship. How can you use what you've learned to enhance your interactions with your partner? Can you think of ways to use this information to increase the satisfaction of both partners in the relationship?

In the space provided, write down how you might behave differently in your relationship as a result of this new information? (Examples: Try to verbalize your feeling more often. Become more understanding of people with traits unlike your own. Move out of your comfort zone by trying a new behavior with your partner. Be more [or less] spontaneous with your loved ones, depending on *their* inner needs.)

_____

Relationships aren't automatic—they require conscious attention.

_____

Part 5:

The Chemistry of Interpersonal Relationships

Introduction

All of your life you've been attracted to certain types of people and repelled by other types. Why is this? Because there are natural affinities between some of the four behavioral traits and static between others. In this part, we'll look at why these exist.

But we're *not* going to give strict compatibility guidelines, suggesting that you only date Dominance people, for instance, or that you avoid Structure types like the plague. Instead, you will learn to assess relationships depending on the mutual goals involved. In a relationship where you are both striving to save enough money to finish college, you may want one kind of mate. If you are happily married, you may be searching for qualities in a best friend that are different from those in your spouse. Or if two people have already attained most of their lifetime ambitions, they may simply be looking for a companion to share their golden years, in which case they might appreciate more fun-loving behavioral traits than they wanted in a partner during their 20s or 30s.

In other words, no outside person can ever really determine the "ideal mate" for you. It's up to you to decide which strengths, energy patterns, and emotional tendencies are most closely aligned with the person you are today—and the person you plan to become tomorrow. Given these caveats, see if you can figure out why you love the people that you do and why other people produce almost instant negative reactions in you, despite your best efforts to be friendly.

Be open to the possibilities of passion—it can give you a new vitality and excitement that is so necessary in our lives today.

Likes Attract—When You're Looking for Comfort

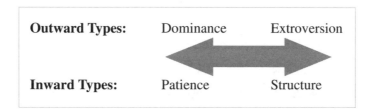

Outward Types:	Dominance	Extroversion
Inward Types:	Patience	Structure

You've heard the old saying that likes attract. This is true—when it comes to social settings and when you want to feel "at home" with another person. That's why you'll find that Dominance and Extroversion types naturally gravitate toward each other. They're both outgoing! And they send out instant signals that broadcast their outgoing nature, such as:

- Being loud, fast talkers
- Giving opinions quickly
- Dressing in a flamboyant or attention-grabbing manner
- Using body language that invites social contact
- Initiating eye contact, and following up by moving into close proximity

Ds and Es are also alike in other habits. They tend to be fast-paced, believing that life's too short to obsess over whether their tires are properly inflated or their socks match their tie. Who's going to care 100 years from now, they ask? They go for the gusto—and are proud of it! And people who don't share these traits seem lifeless, boring, and wimp-like in comparison.

A similar camaraderie exists among the more reserved types, namely people who are highest in Patience and Structure. An unspoken bond unites these people, through behavior like:

- Speaking quietly and waiting their turn in a conversation
- Considering an issue before giving an opinion
- Dressing in a conservative manner, to avoid excessive attention
- Being timid or cautious when meeting other people
- Avoiding prolonged eye contact until an intimate, trustworthy relationship has been established.

People who are highest in P or S want to be around people who won't embarrass them. They don't like surprises, so they find stable, predictable relationships to be most satisfying. This explains why they're not typically comfortable with people who ask deeply personal questions during the first meeting, tell loud or outrageous jokes, or honk their horns in car tunnels.

Compatibility Predictors

In general, you will be most comfortable in social settings where people have the same highest trait that you do: E with other Es, P with Ps, S with Ss. These combinations reinforce our self-esteem, because we do not have to explain ourselves; the other people naturally think the way we do!

Ds flock together, too, but only for a while. Due to their strong competitive streak, they are not quite as harmonious as other groups.

The next level of compatibility is with people who share your inner- or outer-orientation, but not your specific trait. Ps do well with Ss, and Ds with Es. Es and Ps also develop rapport easily, because they both tend to value a positive outlook, and they both aspire to a mutually supportive relationship. It works because the Patience person adopts the giving role, and the Extrovert assumes the role of receiver.

The *least* compatible combinations are between:

- Dominance and Patience
- Dominance and Structure
- Extroversion and Structure

To the Dominance type (who just wants to get things done), and to the Extroversion type (who just wants to have fun), cautious Structure and steady Patience people can be drags. Structure behavior is particularly irritating to Ds and Es, who think that if you pay too much attention to standards and judgments, you're serving time, not living!

Viewed from the opposite perspective, Patience people may resign themselves to the pushiness of Ds and Es, but they're not happy about it. And the Structure types would rather be left alone than have to tolerate excessively D or E people.

Other Types of Behavior Feel Foreign

When a Dominance or Extroversion person meets someone less outgoing, they feel uncomfortable, because they are not receiving "signals" that are instantly recognizable to them. Cautious individuals may appear cold or aloof to someone more outgoing. They also might come across as lacking in self-esteem or powerless (and therefore, to a High D, unimportant). Or their reserve may be perceived as criticism and immediate turn-off to more gregarious types.

But Patience and Structure people feel an equivalent discomfort when around Dominance and Extroversion people, who frequently seem egotistical, bossy, and immature. That's because Ps and Ss define "good" or "acceptable" behavior as being demure and respectful. The bragging or the instant-buddy bonds common between Ds and Es can be downright offensive to inward types, and they may wonder why their more outgoing colleagues don't simply "grow up."

In some respects, however, having relationships with people who are *too* much like you can be boring or lead to unpleasant rivalry. Two High Ds will butt heads for the leadership position. Two High Es will both struggle for center stage. Two High Ps will bliss out together, but not get much accomplished. And two High Ss will become enmeshed in a never-ending debate over the correct way to squeeze a toothpaste tube.

Our most valuable interpersonal relationships are therefore a complex blend of similarities and differences. Our most durable relationships, though, are those based on shared values: where we both believe in the same goals and in the best way to attain those goals. Whether our spouse is more or less talkative than we are is really of much less importance in the long run than whether we agree on general principles, such as "work before play."

The success of a relationship is ultimately determined by shared values, not shared behavioral traits.

Opposites Attract—When You're Looking for Stimulation

Another thing to remember is that while we feel *comfortable* with people like us, we are *stimulated* by people who are different. This explains why we often fall in love with people radically unlike us: they provide that mysterious "spark" of the unknown, which intrigues us during the first few dates, bewitches us during courtship and then often causes us to wonder why we made such a nonsensical choice once we're married. Here's a case study that illustrates the point:

Bryant has a rather unusual SAS profile, in that he is extremely high in both Structure and Extroversion, with a moderate amount of Dominance, and almost no Patience at all. His live-in girlfriend Colleen is almost the mirror opposite: a pure P.

During their first few dates, Bryant dazzled Colleen with his perfectly appointed beachfront condo. He had the latest styles in furniture, from the city's most elegant stores. The artwork gracing the living room was carefully selected to blend with the ocean view. There was not a speck of dust anywhere, or so much as a pencil or paper clip out of place. The condo looked like something out of a magazine, and clearly demonstrated Bryant's stability, sense of order and domesticity. On the down side, he also talked nonstop, making Colleen wonder whether he was more interest in learning about her or in himself.

Bryant didn't seem to notice that Colleen didn't have a chance to say much. In fact, he was very impressed with her listening talents, and assumed that she was equally enamored of him as he was of her. He proceeded to pursue her with single-minded devotion, sending flowers, calling daily, and finally convincing her to move in.

But Colleen has always had doubts about the relationship, and therefore changes the subject every time the conversation rolls dangerously close to marriage. For one thing, the perfectionism that she admired in Bryant's beautiful condo is starting to grow old. Colleen simply isn't very good with the details of housekeeping, and she doesn't want to waste her time fretting about a little spot here or there. She kind of misses the friendly disarray of her apartment, in fact, and would much rather spend time volunteering at the literacy board than scrubbing the tub with a toothbrush.

Another issue for Colleen is the overall talking-to-listening ratio in her conversations with Bryant. She keeps waiting for her turn to speak—and it never seems to come. There's never a pause long enough for her to gather her thoughts and insert an idea or comment. So she ends up feeling discouraged and disempowered by the sheer amount of Bryant's talking, and feels exhausted after an evening alone with him.

Oddly enough, these were the same traits that drew her to Bryant in the first place. She found the order in his life refreshing. She enjoyed having him take charge of their discussions. Perhaps most of all, she liked being able to "make him happy," first by giving him the attention and approval he seemed to need so much, and later by agreeing to live with him.

Is marriage a good idea between Bryant and Colleen? It depends. If they both want to live within their emotional comfort zone, it would be better for them each to find a more similar partner. On the other hand, if they both want to grow and become more flexible, marriage might be an excellent plan—particularly if they can decide on mutually acceptable goals.

Let's say that they both want to live in Southern California, have no more than two children, raise their kids as Buddhists, remain monogamous the rest of their lives, save up for a vacation home, and balance career and family, with both Bryant and Colleen working full-time. Going even further, they agree that money should be saved for a rainy day, it is important to support the church, they will care for their parents through old age, they will pay off credit card charges every month, and they will not cheat on their taxes.

All of the above are major value issues. With consensus on these and other fundamentals, Bryant and Colleen may be able to overcome their differences in Extroversion and Structure traits.

Compatibility From Positive Energy

Another key element for a successful relationship is that both partners are positive and goal-oriented. With positive energy, natural differences can fuel attraction, and help you learn from one another's strengths. On the other hand, if a person is fear-driven, they become judgmental and defensive about opposite styles—the death knell for joy in a relationship. It's all in your attitude!

Let's discuss what could happen if Bryant and Colleen take a conscious look at their behavioral differences, and decide to get married anyway and grow together over the years. It could be very good for each of them. Bryant, a High S, would learn to temper some of his inflexibility, learning that there are many "right" ways to accomplish any task. Some of his sharper edges could come off over the years by incorporating Colleen's Patience in his personality, and trying to adopt her "wait-and-see" attitude. In fact, he will be a much more affectionate (and re-laxed) parent if he follows her lead with children they might have together.

Try something new often so you can continue to learn and grow.

Colleen, for her part, will become a fuller person by letting some of Bryant's S and E rub off on her. She'll become more careful about her finances, and may even balance her checkbook for the first time in her life. She'll start asserting herself in conversation, sticking up for herself more frequently, and learning new social skills that will be useful in her career and various volunteer activities. But these things will only happen if she decides to learn from the decision, rather than feeling hurt or pushed around by Bryant, and accepts his behavior as a possibly positive model.

What if a Dominance person and a Patience type decide to embark on a long-term, committed relationship? If they both maintain a healthy outlook and strive to grow together, the D will slow down, become more mellow, and take more time when making decisions. The P will emulate new Dominance strengths, becoming more assertive, taking charge of situations, and accepting appropriate risks. They both become fuller, more versatile people, who are able to cope positively with a wide range of circumstances and people.

Or if an E and an S are paired, equally valuable lessons can be learned. The Extrovert can become more sensitive and acquire new levels of discretion. The Structure person has an opportunity to become more relaxed and sociable, letting go of fearful reactions and discovering an enhanced enjoyment of life through interactions with other people.

The most difficult trait combination to "make work" is with a high Dominance and a high Structure couple, because both have strong needs for personal control. And neither is accustomed to yielding control. The result is endless bickering and struggles to be "boss." In order for the relationship to succeed, both the D and the S must budge. The Ds must give the Ss the space they need to comply with their inner sense of "rightness." And the Ss must learn to be much more direct and open about their concerns, so that issues can be resolved rationally and fairly.

If you want a comfortable (but possibly boring) relationship, select a partner with your own highest behavioral trait. If you want to be challenged and grow (but possibly feel frustrated, angry, or misunderstood), select a partner with an opposite trait.

COMBINATIONS LEAST LIKELY TO SUCCEED

	Worst	May Be OK
Dominance and:	S, D	P
Extroversion and:	S	P
Patience and:	D	E
Structure and:	D	E

Notice a pattern? Ss and Ds tend to be most difficult to get along with in relationships, due to their need to impose their will or exert control. Ps and Es tend to be easier, because of Ps easygoing nature and Es intuitive social skills. But ANY combination can be a happy one if both people work toward compatibility.

Task-Oriented Relationships

Which of your friends would you rather be stuck with in an elevator for eight hours? Which would you rather depend on for survival on a desert island? More than likely, two different people came to mind. That's because we require different behaviors from others, depending on the objectives we're currently facing.

Often task-oriented relationships work very well when people have differing behavioral styles. "Like" types tend to compete or create conflict, because they have similar needs. Opposites can help us get the job done, because they see possibilities that never occur to us.

A marriage or any other long-term relationship is partly about rapport (requiring behavioral similarities) and partly about tasks (involving behavioral differences). You want a mate who understands your deepest feelings, who knows what makes you "tick." Only another person with similar traits can do this easily. But at the same time, you unconsciously want a mate who can compensate for your weaknesses: change the oil in the car, cook a pie, select mutual funds, coach the kids' soccer team, or plant daffodils in the garden (depending on which of these things you are not very good at). The same thing happens in emotional or mental characteristics. If you fly off the handle, it's probably wise for you to find a partner who stays level-headed. If you're too driven and have a hard time relaxing, you may select a partner with less self-discipline.

The question here is: What is the goal? With each relationship you get a different "mix" of similarities and differences. If there are too few similarities, you feel that the two of you have nothing in common. If there are too few differences, you feel no fascination or allure.

You'll also notice that you are a slightly different person in every relationship, depending on the relative intensity of your partner's traits. This makes sense, because every relationship has a different understood purpose, even if it is never articulated. If your best friend is a Low E, you'll become more talkative. Around your wife, however, who is a Pure E, you will be much quieter. In a group where the other people have low Dominance, you might jump in as the leader. But this Dominance is exchanged for increased Patience when you get home and try to deal with two unruly teenage daughters.

Rules of Thumb For Good Task-Oriented Relationships

1. Realize that resources, rewards, time, space, and attention are often limited commodities. Figure out ways to allocate them fairly.

2. Make certain that both people *feel* that their needs are being met. (This is not at all the same as you determining that someone else's needs are met). If not, tension and conflict will result.

3. Look out for people who need to "win." If you're one of these people yourself, beware that others may feel short-changed and will resent you.

Task-Based Compatibility

When tasks are agreed upon, either consciously or unconsciously, behavioral trait compatibility lines up differently than in social relationships. The most workable combinations in this arena are: S with P; D with P; and E with P. If you want to get a job done, pick someone who is high in Patience.

Why is the Patience everyone's favorite? Because they get along with everyone. They smooth out the disharmony in life. They exert a stabilizing influence with their supportive, calm demeanor. They're genuinely interested in others, and in making a contribution, and they want to be productive partners. For company in an eight-hour elevator stay, they're the hands-down winners.

The second-best combinations for task-oriented relationships are: S with S; S with E; and P with P. Structure looms large here. They may not be as easygoing as the Patience folks, but they are very sensitive to other's feelings and have a passion for excellence. They're wonderfully loyal. They may not be a lot of laughs, but they do an excellent job at anything they commit to. So while the Structure person may be among the *least* desirable in a social setting, they're among the *most* desirable for achieving superior-quality results.

The worst combinations are: D with D; D with S; D with E; and E with E. This might be puzzling, because Dominance is fairly compatible with other types in a social context, as is Extroversion. But their competitive nature and need for control can stymie cooperation, making living arrangements problematic. Two Ds together clash over leadership roles. With a D and an S, the Dominance need for speed and control is frustrated by the Structure need for systematic progress and quality. Two Extroverts guarantee a great party atmosphere, but are amazingly unproductive when working on tasks, as neither is motivate to deal with details. Overall, Ds and Es both know how to create social rapport, but they want to delegate instead of completing duties themselves and become angry or disappear when performance is required.

Fight or Flight When Relationships Fail

Performance issues or other forms of stress often induce a fight-or-flight reaction in all four behavior types, but in slightly different ways. If two Dominance types disagree, their relationship may dissolve into a state of war. With a High D—High E couple, the Extrovert will traipse off in another direction, seeking solace for a bruised ego, while the D storms around in a huff. Patience and Structure people will bump up against each other or against people from the other two groups. Being more inward and less direct, they may not exhibit their feelings. Patience types will hide in their work and put off feeling their emotions until they seem "processed" and inoffensive enough for general consumption. Structure types will plot ways to "get even." This quiet form of revenge may involve withholding information, being unavailable when help is needed, or other demonstrations of passive aggression.

Chemical Reactions: How to Resolve Conflict

But don't lose hope. Yes, there are inherent difficulties among all of the behavioral types. And there are also techniques you can use for reaching a middle ground in conflict situations, so that both people in a relationship feel like winners—and want to continue the relationship.

Two High Ds

Problem: People with high Dominance traits do not care how strongly they come across to each other. They are critical of others and do not want to know the details, only the big picture. They can be very blunt and may even enjoy this bluntness in another High D (unless one has an unfair advantage, such as a superior title). People with Low D observing their interactions may be devastated by the cut-throat nature of their conflict.

Resolution: Two High Ds can build a successful relationship if they agree on mutual goals and utilize their competitive drive to attain these goals. They will need to formalize who makes final decisions, however, to avoid futile power struggles, and should both make an effort to recognize and appreciate the other's contributions. "You drive to the party because you're better at navigating the traffic, and I'll drive back, because I don't drink."

High D with High E

Problem: The person with a High D always wants to maintain control of the situation and may use force, cruelty, illegal, or immoral means to keep it. Ds terseness often feels offensive to the E. But the High E person is not direct and has a hard time getting to the point. This, in turn, drives the D crazy.

Resolution: These two types should avoid pitting themselves against one another, because both are very strong individuals, and arguments are likely to be brutal. Instead, they should make every effort to concentrate on their shared goals, using the Ds technical strengths to enhance the E's people-skills. "You pick out the best features in a new computer, and I'll schmooze the salesperson. That way we'll get the best deal."

High D with High P

Problem: The High D is a tough driver and may not give specific instructions to the High P partner (though expecting miracles). The High P likes a strong leader and wants to plan actions carefully and methodically.

Resolution: These two types can relate very well together, with the D in charge. They should mutually establish time frames, giving the P enough time to feel comfortable and giving the D bottom-line results. "I'd like to take our vacation in Hawaii this year. Is four months enough advance time for you to get used to the idea?"

High D with High S

Problem: This relationship has some built-in difficulties. High Ds don't realize how strongly they come across to others or that they seem overly critical. High Ss perceive the D's demands as personal attacks. Also, Ds do not care about details and only want to know the big picture. Ss want to check every little detail and to do things themselves to assure that they're done "right."

Resolution: A positive relationship can be established if procedures are explained thoroughly to the S. On the other hand, the D person will not tolerate too much in the way of fussiness and will need a certain amount of slack when it comes to performing highly detailed tasks. "You load the dishwasher and I'll empty it, and I'll do my best to put the plates in order just the way you like them."

Two High Es

Problem: Put two high Es together, and they'll both act impulsively. The "heart-over-mind" orientation will fuel the same trait in the other, with little logic entering the picture. They will expend a lot of energy generating new ideas, but they will move on to discussing a new concept before anything comes of their brainstorming.

Resolution: Vow to define—and stick to—objectives and deadlines. Each High E must help the other comply with time frames, or else the relationship will run aground on the practicalities of life. "Let's both make sure that we've paid the mortgage on time this month, so we don't get hit with that darned penalty charge again."

High E with a High P

Problem: What Es want most is a wide circle of friends, and to achieve this end they will tend to exaggerate. But Ps prefer smaller, more intimate groups, where conversation is sincere and realistic. They may therefore feel that the High E is too flashy and not trustworthy.

Resolution: These two types are naturally quite compatible when it comes to resolving conflict, as they both appreciate a congenial atmosphere and are good at coordinating with other people. "It's really no big deal," they might both remark when they see a discussion turning into an argument.

Two High Ps

Problem: This is probably the most compatible of all relationships, because Patience people dislike conflict and do everything they can to avoid it. They exercise utmost care for each other's feelings and avoid pressure. But they are also prone to procrastination, may have problems completing projects, and can spend a considerable amount of time engaged in small talk.

Resolution: A High P couple should agree on pace, goals, and deadlines. They may need help with this from an outsider, as they might procrastinate even on their goal-setting activities. Also, Patience individuals need to learn to consider their own objectives now and again and be certain that they are not being too "polite." Overlooking their own needs will lead to a deterioration in the relationship sooner or later. "Is it good for you?" "I don't know. Is it good for YOU?" "Hey, I asked first . . ."

High P with a High S

Problem: The Patience people are easygoing and don't take life as seriously as their Structure partner. The Structure people are compulsive about details and in determining right from wrong. It's essential to them that things be done correctly. Conversely, the P may not even believe that a yardstick exists for judging.

Resolution: A very successful relationship can be created if these two people agree on a system, which will provide both of them with priorities and possible strong external leadership. This might come from a church, philosophy, environmental commitment, or child-rearing approach. "Whatever the Pope says, we'll go with it."

Two High Ss

Problem: Both Structure partners will believe that they're right, because they live by an inner rule book. They want to do things the way they've always been done. But each comes from a different family of origin, and the rule books and traditions almost never match perfectly. Also, although Ss are highly sensitive to criticism, they don't mind dishing it out.

Resolution: Simply understanding the "proprietary rule book" issue goes a long way toward establishing a good relationship between two Ss. They must also bite their tongue when tempted to find fault with their partner, or else they're liable to get as good as they give. "Your mom folded the towels in half, and mine folded them in thirds. Let's agree on halves in our house, the way you want. But I get to say which way to load the toilet paper roll, okay?" (And avoid saying that anyone who loads the roll outwards is obviously culturally deficient.)

A Better Life Through Chemistry

One very important use for this information about the "chemical" interactions between behavioral types is in assessing (and making progress toward) your "life task." Many people believe that we have specific lessons to be learned in this lifetime, or, at the very least, lessons that we work on during particular phases of our life.

For example, during your student years you may be trying to "find yourself." This requires boldness, experimentation, and a certain amount of assertiveness. But once you become a parent, you need to access new caring skills. For 10 or 20 years, your life will revolve around serving others, being available to them to meet their needs, and generally putting aside many of the items on your personal agenda in order to further the goals of your children.

Beyond these time-limited tasks, you will probably notice that certain life lessons keep presenting themselves to you, no matter where you find yourself. You might have problems dealing with authority, and this issue crops up with your parents as a child, in school, and on the job as an adult. Or maybe it's so hard for you to make decisions that you consistently let the most promising opportunities pass you by. Perhaps you have an uncontrollable temper that causes you to lose relationships and jobs that are of great value to you. Or it might be that an eating disorder, chemical addiction, or chronic lack of energy has plagued you throughout the years.

Take a moment now to consider your "life tasks" as well as the particular "phase tasks" you are currently tackling during this era in your life. Does the chemical potential in your interpersonal relationships help or hinder you in the accomplishment of these tasks?

Blanca was the single mother of two young boys, struggling to make ends meet, when she began dating Carlos. A calm, gentle person herself with very High P traits, there was something in Carlos that she found irresistible. Part of it was his exuberant energy, his willingness to take charge, and his eagerness to be a parent to her sons, indications of his

High D trait. She felt like she was being rescued when they got married. After all, she was so tired of making all the decisions herself and carrying the burden of the entire household on her own shoulders.

But soon after the marriage, Carlos' Dominance behavior began to border on abuse. He shouted frequently at the top of his voice, became angry over the smallest excuse, and eventually began shoving and slapping both Blanca and her sons. Blanca lacked the inner strength to stand up to him, as she always seemed to be suffering from one mysterious ailment or another—ailments that she had never experienced before the marriage. Finally, on the advice of her mother, Blanca went to a domestic violence counselor and joined a weekly support group. This led her to think about the "life tasks" that she, Carlos, and the boys had each brought to the relationship.

At the risk of oversimplification, one of Blanca's life tasks is most likely to get over being intimidated by other people, especially men. She allows them to take advantage of her, even to the point of harming her children, and internalizes her despair by becoming sick, rather than taking appropriate action. She can learn this life task with Carlos; in fact, he may be a perfect "instructor" for this particular lesson, as he does truly love her, and wants to continue their marriage.

But she must put her foot down firmly before conditions get out of hand. This will require that she develop new interpersonal skills. It will also require an investment of energy, learning new behavior patterns that at first feel foreign and uncomfortable. Blanca is the only person who can decide whether she still feels safe enough with Carlos to "learn" these skills with him. She may opt to separate from him, to give herself and her boys some time for emotional healing before she starts the process over again with someone else. Sooner or later, however, she will have to come to grips with the assertiveness issue—whether it's with a husband, boss, neighbor, or other relationship partners.

Carlos faces a very different life task, namely that he must learn to control his temper. Secretly, he feels ashamed of the way he has treated Blanca and her sons. But at the same time, he has lost respect for her over the years because she does not insist that he treat her properly. He justifies his behavior with her, saying that she must have wanted to be treated harshly, because she never stopped him. When he began shouting, she wouldn't tell him to shut up. If he pushed her gently or threw something at her, she didn't push or throw things back. He is accustomed to people setting limits with him, and when they don't, it is hard for him not to abuse his power.

Carlos really wants Blanca to help him be a better person by refusing to be a victim of his anger. The energy that he will expend in controlling his temper is minuscule compared to the energy he wastes during his explosions. In order to get her to stay with him, though, he will have to invest a lot of effort into proving to her that he is a good risk, and that he sincerely wants to work through his anger life task once and for all.

To figure out whether a relationship offers you an acceptable arena for working out a life task, perform some simple mental arithmetic. First, determine whether this is a life task that you are currently prepared to face. If you're barely surviving mentally, physically, economically, or spiritually, then perhaps you need a more supportive relationship that is not quite so challenging. On the other hand, you might be tired of making the same mistakes over and over and are truly ready for a change. If so, then assess how much the other person pushes you out of your comfort zone. Is it a gentle nudge? Or is it more like a rocket blast? Is this the intensity that you really want?

Also try to figure out if you have the inner reserves to succeed. No sane person would set across the desert without sufficient water or begin a week-long backpacking trip without adequate food. In

Blanca's case, we might ask whether she has enough resolve to create a new start with Carols, steadfastly standing up to his anger while she practices her new assertiveness techniques. If not, she and her children will most likely end up in a shelter for battered families. If yes, she has an opportunity for re-establishing a good, productive marriage.

When considering working on a life task in a relationship, ask yourself: Is the time right? Do I have the inner reserves? Will it cost more emotionally than I'm willing to expend? Is this person worth the investment?

Use your knowledge about the predictable issues between behavioral types to perform a "chemical analysis" of your relationships. Too much heat, and you'll both go up in smoke. Too little stimulation, and you'll both stop evolving inside. Balance the amounts of similarities and differences in your behavioral profiles through compromise, negotiation, and thoughtful discussion with your partner—and see how much hidden potential you can find in your relationship!

Your next step is to incorporate what you've learned into your interactions. In the previous case studies, we looked at some ways to communicate with people who are high in Dominance, Extroversion, Patience, and Structure. Part Six elaborates on several basic techniques for clear and effective communication. You are given exercises to determine your current communication style, and then you will learn new ways to send and receive information that will increase understanding in your interactions with each other.

As you consider this new perspective on human behavior, it is important to remember that there are no "ideal" behaviors. When beginning to grasp some of the underlying subtleties of human interaction, the mechanics of effective communication become less mysterious.

Part 6:

Communicating

Part Six: Communicating

Introduction

Perhaps the most significant factor in maintaining a good relationship, or the main pitfall in a bad relationship, is one's ability to communicate.

Clear communication is the glue that holds families together and keeps friendships strong. Communication can literally create, nourish, infect, or destroy a relationship. It is therefore impossible to have a successful, long-term relationship if you and your partner cannot learn to communicate with one another.

We have a whole array of communication methods to choose from, and the quality of a communication has nothing to do with the quantity of words spoken. In fact, it's impossible *not* to communicate—even your silence says something.

It's not just what you say , but *how* you say it.

Take a look at the following ways people communicate and consider how you use these communication styles in your relationships and everyday interactions with others.

Behavioral Communication Styles

Dominance People

Dominance individuals have an authoritative style. They like to "tell" others how it is. Forceful, outspoken and frank, they prefer to say things only once and get impatient if asked to provide too many details. They are not at all afraid to make waves and are generally comfortable with a certain amount of discord. They like to hear clear, concise messages.

So, if you are a Dominance person yourself, you will need to beware of coming on too strong and overpowering others. You will especially need to remember to be tolerant—since about three quarters of the world's population is not governed by your behavior style. To meet your goals for success in a relationship, you will have to take extra effort to accommodate other behavior styles during communications.

Communicating with Dominance People

If you're talking to a High D person, get to the point. Use action statements such as "Let's go to the 9 p.m. show at the Paramount tonight." Be prepared then to be ready to leave on time and know what show you are going to see. Avoid talking about subjects not directly related to the topic at hand and don't be cloudy about issues. Be direct and to the point. Also, be willing to stick to your position; remember that High Ds respect others who demonstrate the courage of their convictions. If they make a remark that rubs you the wrong way, try not to get offended. Remind yourself that these individuals are brusque by nature and they likely don't intend to hurt your feelings.

Extroversion People

Extroverts will try to "sell" you on their concepts, even during ordinary conversations like at the dinner table. They love to talk and are very empathetic. They are more sensitive than High Ds to other behavioral types and intuitively know how to alter their communication style to please others with differing styles.

If you are an Extrovert yourself, be careful not to annoy the Dominance types, embarrass Patience people, or intimidate Structure individuals with your friendliness. Try to "tone it down" until you are certain that your exuberance is appropriate and not putting a partner off.

Communicating with Extroversion People

To communicate effectively with High Es, provide a warm and friendly environment. Never be harsh or insulting. Instead, voice approval of their position and flatter them, because they thrive when appreciated. Ask them feeling questions such as, "Are you happy with the way our vacation plans are coming together?" This type of inquiry will draw out their opinions and comments.

Usually, though, getting Extroverts to talk is not the problem. You will probably have a harder time keeping them on track with the conversation because they will want to keep adding side topics and continue talking beyond the subject at hand. This makes communications with Extroverts tricky because they do not like others controlling the conversation and aren't comfortable with too many facts or abstractions. A good tactic is to jot down details for a later conversation and work on building rapport during each communication.

Patience People

Patience people are relaxed, yet reserved. Their easygoing attitude makes them adopt a "wait and see" approach when confronted with decisions. You can't rush someone high in Patience! Give them time to adjust to anything "new." This is why Patience individuals sometimes begin conversations with comments that seem completely irrelevant; they are trying to buy a little time to allow themselves to feel more settled and adjust to the various personalities present. You can also count on them to notice how other people are feeling and to make efforts to smooth the waters when they perceive conflict coming.

High Ps need to be aware of their tendency to withdraw and counteract it in relationships or social settings. They often assume that others can read their minds or, at a minimum, their body language, and understand them. Instead, the Patience person should make a concerted effort to verbalize feelings, contribute ideas to a partner freely, and take a stand before communication becomes ineffective or gets out of control.

Communicating with Patience People

The best way to talk with High P people is to be considerate of their internal time frame. Begin conversations with a personal comment. This not only breaks the ice, it also allows them to adjust to your communication style. Patience people are extremely "in touch" with the behavioral types of others because they always want harmony.

At all cost, avoid questions that threaten the Patience person. Don't pressure them to justify their feelings or they will simply withdraw and the communication will end. They respond much better to soft requests. A useful strategy for gaining their support is to demonstrate to them how a particular action will create more happiness in the relationship or will benefit others. Elicit their help; this is much more effective than appealing to their self-interest.

If you want to get their opinion, ask them questions such as, "How do you see us doing the remodeling of the kitchen now that we are ready to begin?" If you sense them turning inward, proceed with gentleness, letting them know you need their help, to draw them back into the conversation again. Also, beware of their tendency to say what they think you want to hear. You may have to convince them that you *really* care about their opinion.

Structure People

Structure people are cautious communicators. Their primary motivator is doing "what is right." They are afraid of making mistakes, even in ordinary conversations with loved ones. They can be very defensive if confronted about something they believe strongly in. Two Structure individuals can typically find no resolution if they have strong differing opinions.

If you are a Structure person, try to remember that not everyone cares about details the same way you do. Sometimes it may be necessary to "give" a little or "bend" for the sake of harmony. Also, impossible as it may seem, others may march to a "different drummer" than you, and it helps a relationship if you can be tolerant of human experiences that differ from your own.

Communicating with Structure People

When interacting with a High S person, once again, the best approach is to build from a respect for the needs of that person—this means working within the High S's framework. Prepare what you want to say in advance so you have lots of details, and be ready to give examples of how your position "works" or is accurate. Bring up situations that set a precedence for your position; Structure people love to hear how something has proved successful before. When asking for something from a High S partner, be very clear about what you want.

Try not to be giddy, casual, informal, or loud around Structure individuals. They are concerned and conscientious by nature and appreciate consideration from those they are in relationship with. They also respect well-organized people—messiness or disorder drives them crazy.

Above all, be careful not to make Structure people feel fearful with critical comments. They will dig in their heels and become totally immobilized. Fear often heightens their sense of perfectionism, which can create a bottleneck in resolving differences.

Flattery Will Get You Everywhere

Actually, flattery doesn't work with all behavioral types, particularly Structure individuals, who are suspicious of insincerity. But genuine compliments do work with people across the board. The trick is to phrase your compliments so that people can receive them and benefit from them, and this depends to a large extent on their predominant traits.

With Dominance people, cut to the chase. Cite their achievements, praise their productivity, and recognize their speed and decisiveness. Thank them for focusing on getting things done. "You really got that waiter's attention in a hurry! I'll bet he never makes you sit around waiting for the check again!"

Extroverts want to hear that they're popular. Stroke them for their natural charisma, personal appeal, and persuasiveness. Heap praise upon them for fun ideas, creativity, and conviviality. "You were the life of the party last night. Everybody was laughing about that Darth Vader imitation you did. No wonder you got first prize!"

You can lay it on fairly thick with both Dominance and Extroversion people without embarrassing them. This is because they sometimes have large egos, which require frequent and ongoing feeding for a sense of inner well-being. Fail to give them the pats on the back they need, and they wither. It's better to err on the side of too-frequent or too-lavish compliments with Ds and Es than the other way around. But don't be too effusive when praising Ps and Ss. They'll treasure a well-deserved comment, but feel mortified or irritated by compliments they don't feel they've earned, or that are given at someone else's expense.

Patience people want to know that they are cooperative. They're proud of their ability to get along with others and maintain close, long-term relationships. Because of their desire for harmony, they enjoy group compliments almost as much as individual ones, and they are able to derive pleasure from positive remarks directed at other people. "The close rapport I notice between you and your daughter is really remarkable. I admire the way the two of you get along, even when you have to discipline her! Maybe you could help me with some ideas for relating better with my son."

To compliment Structure people, admire the quality of their work or their organizational skills. Appreciate their thoroughness, precision, and efficiency and point out their conscientiousness and persistence. Avoid excessive praise at all costs. "The bookshelf you built is a truly professional job. Every joint perfect! And you got it done all in one afternoon. Amazing!"

Be conservative when praising Ps and Ss. Be sure that you draw positive attention to their relationships and accomplishments, rather than to their personalities, or they will scoff at you.

With any of the four behavioral types, an affectionate remark or gesture is often even better than a compliment. "I consider you to be one of my best and most valued friends," is often better received than "You're so popular and handsome." The former is an "I" statement, expressing your honest emotions. The second is really a sugar-coated judgment, in which you imply that you're capable of determining whether or not your partner is worthy of general respect and admiration.

When Your Partner is Troubled

Similarly, you need to select the right approach when your partner seems out of sorts and you want to help. Keep these rules of thumb in mind if you want to be a better peer counselor:

- **Dominance people have to feel like they're in charge**. They can't understand (and don't like) vagueness or excessive emotion. So get them to talk by sticking to the facts and allowing them to save face. "I heard on the radio that your company's stock went down today. It must have made people really concerned at the office. What do you think your role will be when you go in tomorrow?"

- **Extroverts want to get it all out**. They process their emotions, both positive and negative, by talking. Often just having a caring listener is enough to make them feel much better. Be prepared to spend a lot of time listening, though, keeping your comments to a minimum. "You haven't seemed like yourself lately. I'm not doing anything special all evening, and I'd be happy to hear what's on your mind."

- **Patience people have trouble figuring out their emotions, and it is hard for them to verbalize feelings on the spot**. So let them take the time they need, even if it's days, weeks or months, to clarify their concerns. Then help them explore their feelings in a completely non-threatening environment. Any angry or judgmental comment and they'll clam right up. "I'm really sorry to hear about your father's passing away so suddenly, and I want you to know that I'm here for you whenever you feel ready to talk about your loss."

- **Structure people want to solve problems through fact-finding and precedent-proving**. You can help them by following a very linear approach, asking detailed questions, and perhaps creating an outline of information gathered. A procedural solution will make most sense to them. "Let's make a list of all the pros and cons of letting Aunt Agnes move in with us and then map out an action plan once we've decided on the best course."

Verbal and Non-Verbal Communication

Verbal and non-verbal communications touch each of us numerous times every day. Have you ever been in a situation where you spoke when you should have kept your mouth shut, or didn't speak and later wished you had spoken your mind? Or have you raised an eyebrow or shaken your head at someone's comments only to have him or her lash out at you for your gesture?

Many times, people fail to say what they really want because of fear—that they'll sound stupid, or hurt someone's feelings or possibly be rejected for their remarks. So they keep silent.

In relationships, partners might avoid discussing differing opinions or desires for fear they might end up arguing. To escape the discomfort of an argument, they might choose to coexist without meaningful communications. This does not strengthen the relationship; it merely creates an uneasy environment where the partners are living with bottled-up anger and unresolved issues.

When you risk the possible consequences of differences and are willing to reveal your true opinions or feelings, and when you learn to communicate in ways that are non-threatening, you will find that your relationships grow stronger and become more satisfying. If you can be open enough to communicate honestly, you can use your differences or disagreements as catalysts for change—both in yourself and in your partner.

Characteristics of Verbal Communication

The following are key elements for communicating effectively:

- Being direct
- Showing respect
- Sharing responsibility
- Having a purpose

Let's review each element in turn.

Being Direct—stating honestly and openly what you want, think, feel, or need

Being direct means being honest and truthful. Being direct both assumes and creates trust. Direct communication is person-to-person. It's timely and candid. You express what you really think and feel—spelling out your views clearly, completely, and constructively.

Being direct is not easy for everyone. But, it comes naturally to High Ds because they like to be clear, specific, brief, and to the point. They do not like to repeat themselves. Because High Ds' forceful, outspoken, frank manner may cause waves or engender conflict, they would be wise to learn humility and acknowledge that their view may not be the only objective truth. High Ds must understand that personal biases will affect how they feel and what they say, but they should not allow this to inhibit their free expression. Being open and freely sharing information and viewpoints is an individual's right, and it is critical to respectfully acknowledge that right for others as well.

If you are low in Dominance by nature, you may have to "push up" on this trait to become a more direct (and effective) communicator.

Showing Respect—honoring another's thoughts, feelings, and opinions

No one individual is entitled to more respect than anyone else. Underlying the notion of respect is the assumption that all people are worthwhile and have a right to their unique experiences and perspectives. Respectful communications require listening and acknowledging the views and feelings of others. This means that their commitments, histories, and values are taken into account in the communication. Respectful interactions may involve disagreements, but they should never involve embarrassment, intimidation, or attacks on the other person.

When you clearly voice your beliefs, you reveal who you really are. This is how you treat yourself as someone who matters, who is worthy of respect.

Respectful communicators interact with others as equal individuals, not as objects. There is a mutual consideration of each other's needs, wants, and viewpoints. This style of communication presents the truth as the speaker sees it—without denigrating the ideas or opinions of others in the process.

Avoid becoming angry or annoyed when another person's views differ from your own. If you do get angry or appear threatened every time someone disagrees with you, people will avoid open communication with you and may be reluctant to be in a relationship with you. Try to understand the other's point of view.

To be a respectful communicator, learn to be more patient.

High Ps have a natural tendency to show respect because of their innate desire for warmth, peace, harmony, and friendly environments. Their data-gathering skill lends itself well to listening and being empathetic to other viewpoints. High Es are also respectful communicators because they do not want to look foolish and they have a strong desire to be liked. Both High Ps and Es naturally interact with others as equals because there is a mutual consideration for the other's needs, wants, and viewpoints.

Sharing Responsibility—ensuring two-way communications that focus on achieving positive, mutually satisfying results

For more purposeful interactions, develop your Dominance trait (so you can see the big picture) and your Structure trait (so you can follow through with the details).

Sharing responsibility in communication is about *not* blaming others. Each person must be committed to the success of the interaction itself and to the results you both hope to achieve. This allows both parties to bring their individual insights and truths to the encounter, knowing that blaming others or pointing fingers is not permitted.

It takes two to communicate, to establish rhythm and mutuality to decide which of you will speak and which will listen and when you will decide to reverse roles. You give your full attention, and you also respect the other's time and possible desire for privacy.

Having Purpose—identifying what you want to accomplish

Purposeful communications are not random; instead, they are focused, intentional, and oriented to specific results. They put information "on the table" that might change the original perspective of others. This may involve gaining a more thorough understanding of the issues or getting a clearer sense of all options, and it will usually require that others be willing to accept a higher level of trust in one another. This is a strength of the High S individual.

The intent in purposeful communication is to get close to an agreement as a result of the interaction. Participants then adjust their actions, words, and feelings as needed to achieve the desired outcome.

Characteristics of Non-Verbal Communication

Although nothing can replace the spoken word, your body language contributes mightily to what you communicate. Some studies indicate that as much as 70 to 93 percent of all communication is nonverbal, such as facial expressions, hand gestures, and body position. Your every movement sends a powerful message. Many times we are oblivious to the nonverbal communication signals we send and equally blind to the ways we automatically react to others, based on our personal interpretation of their non-verbal behavior. Meanings implied by non-verbal communications are often ambiguous because each individual is likely to interpret a non-verbal clue differently. This is why body language is so useful—it allows us to express shades of meaning that might otherwise be lost with words.

There is really no sure way to measure the effect of a non-verbal message in the communication. Suffice it to say, then, that it's critical to pay close attention to each grin, scowl, shrug, eye flicker, and posture that you receive or give, because each sends a message that colors the meaning of the overall communication. A shift in posture or gesture usually points to a corresponding change in the tenor of communications.

Verbal and non-verbal communication is a dynamic and interactive process between two (or more) people. Think of it as a dance. How easily you move depends on the skill level of both you and your partner. If your partner is obviously more skilled, don't feel bad. Perhaps you can relax and follow that lead.

To become a better non-verbal listener, notice what point in a conversation people's gestures or postures shift. This is your cue that a change has occurred in the interpersonal dynamics.

How Do You Communicate?

To evaluate your existing communication skills, ask yourself the following questions:

- Do you put aside your fears and communicate honestly and openly, saying what you really think and feel?
- Do you consider the needs, wants, and view points of others?
- Do you treat your partner as a unique individual?
- Do you try to embarrass, intimidate, or correct your partner?
- Do you share your unique insights and perspectives?
- Do you accept the right of your partner to respond to your opinions and perspectives?
- Do you put aside your fear and accept direct, honest, and open interaction?
- Do you listen intently to the message being stated to understand the view point of your partner?
- Do you listen to and acknowledge the views and feelings of your partner, treating him or her as an equal?
- Do you try to embarrass, intimidate, correct, or attack your partner when he or she criticizes or disagrees with you?
- Do you see communication as an exchange for which you share responsibility?

Receptive vs. Expressive Communications

Receptive communication happens when you receive information without immediately evaluating it at the time of the interaction. *Expressive* communication occurs when you contribute information and direction to the interaction. Both are essential for good interpersonal relationships.

- **Observing**
- **Listening**
- **Empathizing**

When you are receptive during communications, you observe, listen and empathize. You assume a relatively passive role, allowing the other person to carry the ball. But you do more than just sitting with ears open and mouth shut. You make conscious choices to set aside other thoughts, block out distractions, and pay attention to the other's ideas, thoughts, and feelings in the communication. You prove that you're listening by pertinent questions and by "mirroring" information back to the speaker. High Ps are naturally very gifted in receptive skills.

Observing

Observing in a relationship requires you to look at what's happening, to detect consequences of actions, and notice whether what is happening is unique or part of a pattern. When you live with someone full time, you have an opportunity to become a keen observer.

The purpose of *observing* is to gather accurate and specific information about behavior, patterns of behavior, and results. You make a genuine attempt to see and hear accurately, resisting the temptation to make assumptions, interpretations, or judgments about the other person. To help you do this, try to be conscious of any positive or negative reactions during the communication and control your urge to form attitudes and judgments about what you are hearing. "She's biting her nails again. I wonder what went wrong for her today at the office."

We hear and forget. We hear, and we remember. When we see, hear, and remember, we understand and succeed.

Also, observe the comfort level of the other. Is that person:

- Stressed?
- Busy?
- Easygoing?
- Friendly?
- Difficult?
- Cautious?
- Annoyed?
- Accepting?

Use your answer to help decide if this a good time to engage in a discussion.

Here are some potential obstacles or biases that may hinder effective *observing*:

- Preconceived reactions (either positive or negative) toward the other affect your interpretation of what is being said. This can cause "selective observing" and can be particularly debilitating to clear communication—when one looks for problems, one typically finds them.
- Reacting to individuals based on preconceptions you have about certain "groups" or "ideas" you believe they represent. This type of bias will cloud your ability to openly receive the information being communicated.
- Projecting your own fears, assumptions, and beliefs onto others. Then, instead of accurately hearing what the other is communicating, you sift what he or she says through your filter of experience, projecting your own motives, feelings, or thoughts into the communication.

These pitfalls will work to destroy clear and open communication. Your best defense is sufficient self-awareness to avoid them altogether.

Listening

Contrary to what many think, listening is an intensely active—not passive—process. It requires *total concentration* on what the other person is saying. It also requires a generous, loving expenditure of energy to understand what others are truly thinking and feeling.

Listening is hearing what is being said, detecting key points, being present, and checking for accuracy. When you listen in a relationship, you need to:

Listening is vital in a sharing relationship.

- Clear your mind of extraneous thoughts and focus on your partner's words and intended meaning.
- Avoid giving advice unless it's requested.
- Paraphrase and ask questions to confirm your understanding of what has been said. This comes more easily when you have a genuine interest in what the other person is saying and/or curiosity about the point of view. Hearing another person's point of view does not require that you agree with it. One way to promote accurate understanding is to respect the other person's feelings and thoughts. A willingness to change your views as new information becomes available is one hallmark of effective listening skills. One of the greatest challenges in relationships is to keep an open mind. "I'd always assumed that domestic cars were best, but I'd be happy to hear why you'd rather buy an import."
- Limit your questions to affirm the other's feelings. "That sounds upsetting. Tell me more about it."

Effective listening requires observing and becoming sensitive to your partner's unspoken feelings, nuances, and emotions. You must also try to understand what your partner wants to achieve from the communication, which is especially difficult if your wants differ. Above all, refrain from interjecting reactions and rebuttals.

Whether you're talking, listening, or being silent with your partner, savor the present moment instead of planning for future events.

Silence can often be a valuable listening tool as well, if your body language continues to send a caring supportive message. People who are low in Extroversion and/or high in Patience appreciate silences, so they can gather their thoughts.

Don't be afraid to allow silences in your conversations, especially when listening to Low Es and/or High Ps.

First listen. Then when you do speak, begin with a compliment. In all exchanges, this is a good way to behave. If you feel you can ask questions to gain information after you have finished listening, do. This saves time for both of you. Try to draw out your partner, and don't try to divert the conversation to yourself immediately. We usually learn most when our mouths are closed. High Es particularly must empty themselves of the need to control the conversation.

Remember that communication is a two-way street! If you are not committed to listening respectfully during a communication, you cannot expect to be listened to with respect either. Give good listening attention, and you'll receive it when it's your turn to talk.

Empathizing

Empathizing is the ability to detect another's feelings and values and validate a common understanding. The Latin root means literally to "feel with." Empathy is so rare that it is valued above all other human traits. High Es and High Ps have this characteristic naturally.

When you have empathy toward your partner, you:

- Acknowledge and accept your partner's thoughts, values, and opinions.
- Communicate your understanding of the other person's thoughts, values, feelings, and opinions.
- Share your experiences to demonstrate your understanding.

Empathizing will reduce tension and improve trust and sharing during the communication.

It is important to share common experiences, feelings, and values, otherwise you can't find common ground or establish mutual trust. Sometimes a nod or gesture is all it takes to demonstrate that you understand and can relate to what your partner is saying. Also, when you exhibit empathy, you create a safe emotional space in common with your partner, where they can let down their reserve, break through their fears, and reach a deeper level of rapport with you.

It may be very difficult to be empathetic when the other person's experiences, feelings, and values are drastically different from your own. However, at the very least, respectfully acknowledging that the other person has strongly held experiences, feelings, and values, maintains open channels for communication.

Now, let's look at the role expressive skills play in the way people communicate.

Being Expressive in Communication—You Are:

- Questioning
- Describing
- Concluding

Expressive skills are invaluable in enhancing clear and open communication. By questioning, describing, and drawing conclusions, you add information and direction to your communication. Consider how the following techniques might improve your communications.

Questioning

Questions facilitate discovery. When you inquire, you ask your partner to clarify information or elaborate on an opinion. This is a wonderful way to prevent misunderstanding and provide time to reflect, which can reduce tension and minimize the risk of jumping to premature conclusions.

No matter how busy you are, set aside time to talk regularly with your partner. Ask such simple questions as, "What was the best part of your day?" or, "Did anything funny happen today?"

Find a way to get genuinely interested in what your partner is saying and express your interest with both verbal and non-verbal cues.

Describing

In a relationship, describing specific examples of actions and behavior you like or dislike during an interaction and discussing the effect of this behavior creates clear communications.

Be clear about what exactly you are seeing and what exactly you are feeling as a result of a behavior, and be clear in describing how what you are seeing and hearing affects your ability to be involved and stay involved openly in the communication. "You know the way you rubbed my shoulders tonight? I just love it when you do that!"

Concluding

The ability to draw conclusions will clarify your overall position and help you make decisions and recommendations. Concluding involves:

- Assessing and determining the overall quality of observed behaviors and their results.
- Controlling personal biases.
- Separating out "what is" in your control from "what is not."

To conclude is to wrap up the interaction/communication with concrete, specific examples to substantiate your evaluations, recommendations, and decisions. When you conclude, you assess the information available in the communication and provide both the criteria for your conclusion as well as the conclusion itself. Whether or not you have reached an agreement, you have the clear responsibility to bring the discussion to a conclusion.

> Example:
>
> Gregory: There was a really funny smell in the back of your car when I bor-
>   rowed it this afternoon. What in the world are you carrying around in
>   it? (Questioning)
>
> Hannah: Oh really? What did it smell like?
>
> Gregory: Sort of like six-month old roadkill. (Describing)
>
> Hannah: Oh gosh, I must have left one of the baby's messy diapers under the
>   seat again. I was in such a hurry on Sunday when I last used the car . . .
>
> Gregory: Well how about if we fish it out and donate it to the archeological
>   society? (Concluding)

Balancing Communications

A healthy relationship needs a balance of communication skills. To review briefly, consider that:

- Being *receptive* and *expressive* shows understanding and consideration of the other's point of view. These skills create mutual respect. This is a natural for High Ps.

- Being *direct* relies on strong expressive skills. This is a natural for High Ds.

- *Sharing responsibility* occurs when both parties in the communication are willing and able to shift back and forth between receiving and expressing. High Es and High Ps naturally understand the need to share in the responsibility of communicating effectively, unless High Es decide to do all the talking.

- *Having a purpose* needs to be expressed and then received before differences can be re-solved. Defining purpose is a natural for High S individuals.

As Emerson wrote, "The only way to have a friend is to be one."

For some behavior types, receptive skills come more easily than expressive skills. And for many, there will be mixed results when first learning to use these skills. To enhance relationships, developing the skill to use a balance of communication techniques requires practice. It all begins with those first attempts, so give it a try.

To create balance, provide an equal courtesy to your partner. If you want your partner to listen carefully to what you say without criticism, then *you* must first listen without criticism. If you want your partner to help you, then you must first offer to help. If you want your partner to try your ideas, express your willingness to try his or her ideas. If you want your partner to excuse your errors, you must be willing to forgive at the same time.

Ultimately we strive for balance.

To create balance in a relationship, when your partner expresses an emotion such as sorrow or anger, respond. Let your partner know that you recognize sorrow, anger, or fear. Say, "You seem to be upset. Tell me what's wrong." Then, express understanding. If you then say, "I see how you'd be upset under those conditions," you will be helping your partner work through those difficulties.

If your partner starts to act confused, upset, or irrational, remain silent and keep a safe distance. As you become a keen observer, you will learn to recognize more subtle irrational actions. Be aware of inappropriate remarks, sarcasm, belittling comments, verbal threats, clenched fists, reddened face, ranting, raving, and physical attacks. These actions are usually the result of some vividly imagined or real danger. Irrational partners are dangerous. Stay out of their way.

To create balance and appreciation in a relationship is to share in your partner's enthusiasm. When your partner shows excitement, respond by saying, "Hey, you really look excited. What's up?" Say "That's great!" to show you care.

Using these balanced communication skills is crucial when you live with someone full-time. It's all too easy to become complacent and think this individual can somehow read your mind. That is likely to never be the case! Instead, relish the opportunity to open up and be open and share. Be a good listener and a keen observer, to encourage your partner to be open and share. Be willing to put in the emotional energy necessary to commit to clear and open communications—the results are well worth the effort. Developing the sensitivity to better understand the feelings, emotions, and values of your partner will provide the depth you both hope to find in your relationship.

PART SIX: COMMUNICATING

Part 7:

*Sharing Yourselves
with Each Other*

Introduction

The more ways you can find to share yourselves with each other, the stronger your relationship will become. Strive to share all areas of life—your time, activities, interests, ideas, spiritual beliefs, family objectives, and goals. Sharing demands that you give of yourself, listen to your partner, and, as your lives entwine, develop a sensitivity to moments that offer possibilities for further exploration to help deepen your relationship.

We share our spirit with others.

Picture it as taking an adventurous journey together where you will discover interesting new territory in each other through the experiences of sharing on successively deeper levels as you walk through life's passages.

Now, creatively evaluate where you can nurture sharing in your relationship. Look at your life together in these four areas:

- **Common ground**. Think of all the things you actually share right now. How can you enjoy them more?

- **Separate ground**. Realize that parts of your life, particularly in the areas of work and responsibility, may be separate. You may also have special interests that your partner will never become directly involved in, such as friends from your childhood or obligations to your family of origin. How can you bridge these gaps so that you can share your separate worlds? You may want to communicate more closely with your partner to achieve mutual understanding through encouragement.

- **New ground for one**. What interests can you begin to enjoy because your partner enjoys them? If you each develop new enthusiasm to match your partner's, life together will become more interesting than ever.

- **New ground for both**. What new, absorbing interests can you develop together? Make a list of fresh opportunities for variety and adventure with your partner, then review it every six months. Create magical moments together. You'll increase your ability to communicate, and you'll discover new adventures that you can experience together.

Private Time Together

Studies suggest that a crucial factor in a satisfying relationship is the ability to share private thoughts and feelings with each other. No matter how busy you are, make an effort regularly to plan private time when you can be together to share, to be receptive, to see and hear what's on each other's mind. Train yourself to listen nonjudgmentally—so you create an atmosphere in which you feel safe to explore the multitude of issues in your lives together. Choose a time to talk when you are both emotionally available, neither of you is exhausted, and your environment is conducive to intimacy and rapport. If you have to, make a date for this private time, and guard the time jealously. Get a baby-sitter. Go on a weekend getaway. Do whatever it takes to make the time special and inviolate.

Schedule private time with your partner on a regular basis so you can relax, be truly attentive, and appreciate the qualities you love most in each other.

Share Your Satisfaction

What is satisfying to you about your relationship?

The following exercise will allow you and your partner to look at how satisfied you are in your current relationship. Use the space provided to write your answers.

Rejoice together.

Exercise 7-1: How Satisfied Are You?

YOU

Make a list of six things you like to do.

1.

2.

3.

4.

5.

6.

Have I done these recently, or do I do them often enough?

What did these cost—and what were the consequences?

Were these planned, or did I do it spontaneously?

What would my ideal life look like?

What would an ideal day in this ideal life involve?

What are absolute essentials in your answer to the last two questions? How can you get those essentials?

Describe the type of environment in your relationship that would allow you to be your true self.

If you had five separate lives, what would they be?

What is really important to you?

List the five things you value most.	Now prioritize their value to you.
1.	1.
2.	2.
3.	3.
4.	4.
5.	5.

Study your priority list, then ask yourself the following questions:

How do the values I've identified relate to my relationship?

1.

2.

3.

Ask yourself, "Does the way I live my life now reflect what I say I value?" Explain.

YOUR PARTNER

Make a list of six things you like to do.

1.

2.

3.

4.

5.

6.

Have I done these recently, or do I do them often enough?

What did these cost—and what were the consequences?

Were these planned, or did I do it spontaneously?

What would my ideal life look like?

What would an ideal day in this ideal life involve?

What are absolute essentials in your answer to the last two questions? How can you get those essentials?

Describe the type of environment in your relationship that would allow you to be your true self.

If you had five separate lives, what would they be?

What is really important to you?

List the five things you value most.   Now prioritize their value to you.

1.   1.

2.   2.

3.   3.

4.   4.

5.   5.

Study your priority list, then ask yourself the following questions:

How do the values I've identified relate to my relationship?

1.

2.

3.

Ask yourself, "Does the way I live my life now reflect what I say I value?" Explain.

From your answers to this exercise, develop new goals for your relationship—goals that will give you a greater sense of satisfaction. What are your goals in this relationship—would you like to set new goals? Goals are the basic targets of life. They spring from our dreams. If you want a relationship of your dreams, you must begin by establishing goals to create that kind of relationship.

Oftentimes, however, greater satisfaction cannot be achieved until you look at the role stress is playing in your relationship.

Share Your Stress

Since the mid-70s, "stress" has become a household word—a catch-all term for what troubles us. The problem is that we approach stress like we approach any other disease. We want to find out what's going wrong and then go out and fix it.

But stress is not at all a disease. It isn't a biological entity like bacteria or a virus, nor does it lurk in dank sewers or contaminated water. Rather, it is a *dis*-ease, an inner imbalance within our bodies and minds. Stress is psychosomatic in the true sense of the word—involving both body and mind. Its source lies in the patterns and habits that make up our lives or in how we regulate (or fail to regulate) our inner resources.

In other words, *we create stress whenever we mismanage our own inner resources.*

A perfect example is provided by Bobbie Ann. When asked, "What is the single most stressful thing in your life right now?" she replied as follows:

> "Trying to juggle being a single mom of two little kids, and working long hours in a big office, and then trying to find time to go out on a date occasionally. I start to cry sometimes for no real reason, just because there's so little time, money, and energy to go around. It gets worse during the holidays, because there are so many things I want to get for my kids and do for them, but can't. It feels pretty hopeless when I look at a whole new year just beginning—a new year that will most likely be just as difficult as the past one."

There are several different ways of looking at stress—and the one given most often is . . . "if only." If only my job were easier. If only my son would do better in school. If only I had more money, or a better job, or a newer car, or a bigger house. Then I'd have less stress, because some of my problems would go away.

Don't let stress erode the excitement in your relationship. Determine whether stress is individual, or created by the two of you together. Then take steps to heal the situation.

But the sad truth is that we really can't fix life. Of course, we can do some minor tweaks that will help a little. But on the whole, life is always going to present us with challenges and difficulties, which will create that unpleasant feeling of stress inside us. Just as soon as we think we've got one problem licked, along comes a new one to take its place, usually the same old problem reappearing, dressed in different clothes.

Take responsibility for your stress. Stop blaming it on the world or your partner. You are not a victim—in fact, you're nothing less than the creator of your own life!

We feel powerless against these outside forces—because we *are* powerless. We can't control the world, so we create myths about stress, which after a while we assume to be the gospel truth.

For instance, one myth says that "Stress is something that happens to me." Certainly there are outside circumstances that are well-documented in creating stress, such as a death or serious illness in the family, a bankruptcy, going through a divorce, or losing a job. It's also fair to say that a single mother like Bobbie Ann faces considerably more daily stress than a millionaire relaxing on a yacht. Nevertheless, we simply cannot blame our stress on circumstance outside of our control, because then we become victims. The very act of seeing ourselves as a victim contributes greatly to our stress level!

The fact is that we are the source of our own stress, because stress can best be defined as our reaction to the things that happen to us. This is both good news and bad, because if we have the power to create stress and unhappiness, we also have the power to create harmony and happiness within ourselves. How? By increasing our self-awareness, and by becoming conscious of the effects that our decisions have on our sense of inner well-being.

There's another very useful way to define stress, and that is the amount of energy we are expending to be someone that we're not. We all have an innate self—basically, the person we were born to be—dwelling inside of us. For one reason or another, most of us live lives of "quiet desperation," as Thoreau put it, because we are trying to be someone else. We're trying to be the person our parents, supervisor, teacher, or spouse want us to be. Often this is well and good, as it creates a stretch inside toward being a more mature and well-rounded human being. But it also creates an energy drain, unless we are completely clear about being committed to personal growth in the relationship. When we are *aware* of an energy drain, or an inner adjustment away from our most natural self, and are making the change willingly, it becomes less stressful to us.

Many people face stress due to destructive patterns and habits, like smoking. It's widely known that the nicotine addiction creates stress on your entire body, both in the short-term and the long-term. But how many of us look on smoking as a contributor to our overall stress and make a firm resolution to quit?

The better we understand the behavioral motivators within ourselves and our partners, the more flexible we can be in our relationships. We learn to reduce tension, sometimes by refusing to deviate from the patterns of our innate self and other times by freely adopting behavior traits that will be more successful.

Some people resist the idea of modifying their underlying style. As Popeye says, "I am what I am, and that's all that I am." We often hear people say, "What you see is what you get. Take me or leave me." A very high scoring in some of the traits, such as Dominance or Structure, makes it very difficult for a person to be adaptable—not impossible, but difficult.

It's not wise to completely modify our basic personality, or try to be someone who we're not, because this can actually *induce* a great amount of our stress. Instead, we should all consider becoming bilingual in our behavioral composition. We learn how to use capabilities from traits that we're not so strong in, so we can act more appropriately in any given situation.

Each behavioral style has its own distinctive way of reacting to stress. We will look at each of the four in turn.

Are you trying to be someone that you're not in order to please your partner or attract a new romantic interest? Take a look at how much stress this may be creating in your life—and decide if this is a price you're willing to pay.

Stress in High Dominance Individuals

We'll begin with Dominance. When people with a lot of Dominance in their make-up feel stressed, they get angry. They blow up. They also become highly critical and aggressive in the way they express themselves. They can appear like dictators to the people around them—pushy, uncooperative, and resistant.

Why do they get this way? Most often because they don't realize that they have a choice. Maybe they had a parent who always got mad when the heat was on. Or they might think that getting angry is the only "manly" way to maintain dignity in the face of problems. Or perhaps they get so overwhelmed with emotion that they can't even consider any alternatives to anger.

Instead of judging this type of response, let's look at WHY Dominance people get angry. It's almost always because their needs are not getting met. Their needs often include bottom-line results, tangible evidence of progress, a fast pace, and a sense that time is being used efficiently. And above all, they desire a feeling of being in control.

Listen to Jennifer describe the stress she feels due to her partner's Dominance trait:

My boyfriend and I had a big fight recently, and now I don't know what to do. He's a policeman, about 10 years older than me. We live together, because we're saving up money to get married in August. I work as a receptionist in a hotel, so I don't make nearly as much as he does.

About two weeks ago, he opened up the closet, and started throwing out his clothes every which way, yelling at the top of his lungs. I went running in to see what was the matter I'd put his uniform shirts next to the white short-sleeved shirts instead of the white long-sleeved when I ironed them. He has a system for the closets, his drawers, and the kitchen cupboards, and even the refrigerator, where everything has to be in exactly the same place all the time.

Afterwards I felt terrible, because he made me pick up all the shirts, and iron everything all over again, which took me most of the day. Also, he made me apologize and promise that I'd never put the shirts in the wrong place again. Above all, I had to tell him that I'd respect his wishes more in the future. He said this incident proved that I didn't have any regard for him as a person, and I didn't respect his authority, and he doesn't want to be married to anyone who doesn't know who was boss."

Jennifer is clearly living with a very high Dominance person. Her boyfriend is quite a bit older than she is, and he earns more money, both of which could give him a certain amount of control over her. In addition, he's a policeman, so he's accustomed to a position of authority, giving orders and being obeyed. That means that from the outset, Jennifer knows that she's got to be fairly firm with this person in order to hold her own. This is not a man who's going to soft-pedal around issues or wait for days while she makes up her mind on a subject. It's also highly unlikely that he will change much before their wedding date, either.

Jennifer would do well to ask herself whether she wants to invest a great amount of energy into "holding her own" and conforming to this man's wishes. Many women would refuse to iron a man's shirts in the first place, especially if both of them work full-time. Similarly, many women would let their partners keep track of his own half of the closet and organize it however he likes. In this way, people can exercise control over their own environment, but not control over their partner's.

Why is control so important to people like Jennifer's boyfriend? Typically, the answer is insecurity. Dominance people don't believe that their needs can ever really be met with someone else holding the reins. To create a sense of safety, they do everything in their power to stay in charge, holding firm for all they're worth.

This creates inner stress, both for the Dominance person and for all the people around them. Dominance people can never relax. They can't trust. And they have to be constantly prepared to defend their position with anger—a stressful proposition in and of itself.

If you recognize yourself in Jennifer's boyfriend, here are a few questions to ponder with regard to stress:

- Are you tired of the Dominance-related stress that you're carrying?
- Do you wish that you could get closer to other people?
- Are you sometimes surprised, and even dismayed, by your angry outbursts?
- Do you want to keep all of your *con*structive Dominance-related traits, like your excellent leadership talents and your ability to see the Big Picture, but let go of the *de*structive ones, like your tendency to get embroiled in clashes with other people?

The anger expressed by very high Dominance people can be harmful, both to themselves and to the people they love. But the answer is not necessarily to stamp down Dominance. Instead, try to temper the trait by increasing Extroversion and/or Patience, for greater compassion and understanding.

The first step in reducing Dominance-related stress is simply to become aware of what's going on. Begin noticing the effects of your less-constructive Dominance behavior and pay attention to the feelings that Dominance-type perceptions create within you.

If you're dealing with high Dominance people, and you notice that they're becoming stressed, there are a number of things you can do to make it easier for them. For one thing, don't do anything to challenge their sense of authority. This doesn't necessarily mean that you let them have their way. But you make it *appear* that they're getting their way, so they can save face, and still feel like the master of the situation.

You can also speed up the pace of things. If you're not high in Dominance yourself, you probably don't charge as quickly toward bottom-line results as Dominance partners would like. So be sensitive to this need, and do your best to hustle—because although a faster speed might increase *your* stress level, it actually helps decrease theirs.

If all else fails, apologize. Dominance people are often instantly appeased by an apology. You can then get things back on an even footing and carry on with whatever your real agenda is.

But you don't have to give in to them all the time, either. Dominance people tend to respect a firm backbone, and they will treat you better in the long run if you demonstrate a good amount of self-esteem. Give them well-considered reasons, and not too many details, without getting into a battle for control, and you'll do just fine.

Stress in Low Dominance Individuals

There are also typical stressors that low Dominance people experience in relationships. Many of these overlap with high Patience traits (often Low D traits are found in people with High P), discussed later in this part. In general, people with low Dominance allow themselves to be pushed around. They often confuse assertiveness with aggression—and they abhor aggression. So they avoid sticking up for themselves, even when it's necessary for their own good.

In a relationship, this can pose difficulties. The low Dominance person may avoid taking a stand, only to find that resentment builds beneath the surface. Giving in is not at all the same as agreeing; and the conflict that this creates generates excruciating inner stress. Self-esteem suffers, and the person feels a debilitating lack of direction. Low Dominance people can become hopeless, too, since they can't see any way out of their plight.

Dominance in a relationship tends to be a relative matter. One person is almost always higher than the other, regardless of whether that person is perceived as High D in the external world. This explains why one person makes most of the decisions in a relationship. The other, lower D person goes along with things, but does not necessarily feel fulfilled or content.

If you are the low D person in a relationship, be aware of whether your deepest needs are being met. If not, be willing to disturb the status quo, and speak up. Realize that establishing your worth and credibility is essential for healthy relationship. Allowing your partner to have his or her way consistently over a long period will cause your relationship to decay, and sooner or later you will be forced to make a major change. So speak your mind. Delve into your emotional world, and share your feelings and desires with your partner. Insist on getting your own way every now and again, just to stay in practice. And vow never to compromise on the issues that represent your core values.

People who are low in Dominance can reduce their stress level by becoming more assertive. Then their relationship partner does not have to "take care" of their inner needs.

Stress in High Extroversion Individuals

When Extroverts feel stressed, they become overeager and impulsive. Like Dominance people, they feel a strong need to exert control over their environment—and they accomplish this by influencing other people with their exuberance. The behavior *seems* friendly and cheerful, but it can also be downright manipulative.

During conflict with an Extrovert, they're likely to confuse you with the skillfulness of their verbal attack. They're experts at talking, and enjoy verbal sparring for its own sake. It's very difficult to pin them down, though, so that real issues can be resolved. Instead, when the heat is on, Extroverts tend to disregard facts and comments made by other people. They see themselves in the spotlight, and it's hard for their eyes to focus on members of the supporting cast or the audience surrounding them.

Extroverts typically feel stressed when they fail to receive the personal attention they want, when they don't feel "affirmed," or when they're not receiving sufficient praise. They want other people to admire them, engage with them, and act as if they care. They want friends, *lots* of them. And they want all of these things expressed in words, preferably in person, with face-to-face interaction.

This means that alone-time can be very stressful to an Extrovert. They grow restless in isolation, or when there is too little social stimulation. They become uncomfortable when they feel "upstaged," when someone is stealing their limelight. They're also very sensitive to criticism, or even the *hint* of criticism, so great is their need to be liked.

Doesn't everybody want to be liked? Of course. And we all have certain amount of Extroversion inside us, some to a greater extent, and some to a lesser extent. No one enjoys being criticized, for that matter, and everyone enjoys affection and affirmation from others. These are common human needs.

Tony describes some of the stress that comes with being an Extrovert:

> I come on strong in everything that I do, and this usually works fine, especially with the kids in the classes I teach in high school. I'm a big hit with the students. But I'm not such a big hit with our introverted principal, who has given me poor performance evaluations that might have a negative impact on my career in the district. In particular, she wrote comments on my behavior in staff meetings, saying that I can sometimes be disrespectful and uncooperative. I would like to know what to do to turn around my relationship with this woman and keep my job relatively secure.

We can examine two main categories of issues between Tony and his principal, namely typical Extrovert stress issues on his part and typical Introvert issues on hers.

Consider a typical staff meeting. As principal, the boss is supposed to be in charge. Yet she is introverted, so she may be slightly uncomfortable leading the meeting. She works hard to overcome these feelings, but still, the most she can exert is a minimal amount of authority. The other Introverts in the group understand, however. They can read her body language and her subtleties, and they are happy to be part of a quiet, orderly, and fairly conservative meeting style.

Extroverts are more flamboyant, though, and Tony, probably finds an Introverted leadership style to be somewhat boring. He wants plenty of action and verbal interchange. He enjoys a chance to consolidate friendships with other staff members and generally get to know his co-workers better. In fact, he would be much happier with a party atmosphere instead of dull staff meetings.

It's also likely that Tony does more than his fair share of talking at staff meetings. Extroverts often lack an inner balance detector to tell them when they're monopolizing the conversation. They also don't realize how offensive their behavior can be to quieter folks. There may be introverted teachers who wait patiently for a break in the conversation, week after week, only to find that these breaks never materialize. The Extroverts have long since grabbed them all up! Perhaps the principal is even one of these people waiting to get a word in edgewise. Maybe she views Tony's talkativeness as a challenge to her authority and feels severely threatened.

Tony's negative evaluations are really about control-related stress. Introverts are not much interested in control. It's hard for them to take the reins and exert their will over other people. When they're forced into this type of situation, whether by family or career or civic responsibilities, they assume the role reluctantly. They expect others to understand this reluctance and be respectful of it by cooperating.

Remember, too, that Introverts are in touch with their inner world and can have a hard time relating to external forces. They're careful and a little formal. Like all of us, they assume that the rest of the human population thinks exactly the way they do.

But such is not the case. Extroverts like Tony are a good case in point. Extroverts are INformal. They shun divisions of labor. They don't like to follow fixed agendas. They like to visit many different topics in quick succession. Above all, they want to work in an environment that is *fun*, and upbeat, and full of lively celebration.

There are several things Tony can try for improving his relationship with the principal. One of the best is to simply become *aware* of what's going on and notice what kinds of issues are pushing his stress buttons at school. Is it just performance evaluations? Is it mostly when he finds himself in a meeting? Or does he feel unpleasantly stressed whenever he has anything to do with the principal?

Next, Tony can evaluate whether an inner or an outer resolution is in order. For instance, let's say he notices that he feels stressed if the principal doesn't praise him every single day. Maybe both of his parents were Extroverts and were lavish in their praise. Maybe he grew up expecting to have an ongoing source of approval from people in authority positions. This would make him unconsciously disappointed whenever his expectations were not being met.

Once Tony knows this, he can decide what to do next. He could have a meeting with the principal and explain how badly he needs her daily approval. Then, if it appears that she is either unwilling or unable to give it to him, he can evaluate whether or not he is willing to continue teaching under her.

Extroverts can reduce their stress level by learning to give themselves the compliments and ongoing approval they seek from other people. This takes pressure off the people they are in relationships with.

He could also look for another source of this approval—maybe from his wife, or a counselor, or some other person who is very generous with affection.

Or, Tony could find new ways to give ongoing praise to himself, instead of waiting for it to come from other people. This frees him, making him more independent, so he can reduce stress on his own, whenever he wants.

Let's say you notice that you talk about twice as much as most of the other people in meetings. Give yourself a mini-assignment during the next meeting—talk only half as much as you normally do. Or you could put it another way—that you'll make only as many comments as one of the quieter members of the group.

Then when you feel the urge to contribute an idea, and you've already used up the quote of time you've allotted yourself, give yourself some silent kudos. "Nice going," you can say to yourself. "You're doing a fine job of letting other people express themselves. I'm proud of the way you're being generous here, and being sensitive to the needs of others. Some day these new skills are going to come in really handy. So keep it up—and surely the stress that's bugging you right now will diminish over time."

This kind of self-talk can be a wonderful source of inner nourishment. Best of all, it can make you bilingual when it comes to behavioral styles. Although you are still by nature an Extrovert, and even though you would love to receive praise every day from everyone you meet, you are no longer *dependent* on it for your well-being. This reduces your stress level significantly, because you've downscaled your craving for attention from being a *need* to a *preference*.

Stress in Introverted Individuals

We can also address Tony's situation from the Introvert's point of view. We'll assume, for simplicity's sake, that Tony's principal is a "classic" Introvert. That means that she likes to think about ideas before she puts them into words. She is cautious in her interpersonal relationships. She doesn't like to practice new things in public, where other people can watch her progress—she prefers to perfect skills in private and then present them polished and shining to the world when she feels good and ready.

Unfortunately for Introverts, one skill that is impossible to polish in privacy is sociability, since being sociable takes some practice. So most likely, the principal does not have the social ease and fluency that the Extroverts on her staff do. She probably worries over things that she's said, fearful of hurting others' feelings and making mistakes. This makes it hard for her to express herself when put on the spot or when new ideas come up and she must respond quickly—like when Extroverts want to get off the subject during a staff meeting.

She's also probably mystified that the Extroverts around her don't pay attention to every word she says. Introverts distill their speech; when they say things, they expect others to understand that they are presenting gems to be treasured. Extroverts, on the other hand, give diamonds in the rough when they speak. They consider conversation to be a tumbler, where ideas become refined. So they don't tend to pay close attention to every comment. They also don't mind repeating themselves or listening to repetitious remarks.

Introverts can reduce stress in relationships by becoming more vocal and stating their desires clearly. This relieves their partners from having to be mind-readers.

So the principal can apply the same advice we gave to extroverted Tony and observe the stress she feels when interacting with Extroverts. Are the Extroverts *trying* to hurt her feelings, challenge her authority, or act as if her agenda is unimportant? No, they are merely behaving like Extroverts. Is she *trying* to appear aloof or cold to the Extroverts on her staff? Not at all; she is simply acting predictably like an Introvert.

Tony's introverted principal may feel stressed by Tony's need for praise. She may feel exhausted by the amount of interaction he wants with her. Bear in mind that the inner battery of Introverts is *drained* by social contact and *recharged* by solitude. Extroverts are just the opposite. Nothing energizes them like being around other people, and nothing makes them depressed like being alone.

Energy drain is another way of saying stress. Whenever we're experiencing energy drain, we need to look at it, and decide if we want to be using our life force in this manner. Maybe yes. Maybe no. Whatever, we notice the fact that we have a choice!

Tony's principal can reduce her stressful energy drain by re-evaluating her working relationship with Tony and other Extroverts on her faculty. Will they respond to suggestions that they "tone it down" during staff meetings? Can she schedule shorter meetings, so that the Extroverts have an easier time staying on task? Can she learn to be more tolerant and supportive of their needs, perhaps hosting a staff party or two every year so that they don't need to socialize on school time? These examples illustrate that there are many things that can be done to achieve a common ground between very different behavioral types and still accommodate everyone's inner requirements.

Stress in High Patience Individuals

When high Patience people feel stressed, they don't explode into anger, as high Dominance people do. Nor do they gloss over problems with optimism, the way Extroverts do. Instead high Patience people internalize their feelings. To an outsider, it may seem like they have no emotions at all. But deep within, moving with the slow but steady progress of a glacier, their feelings are taking form and digging deep into their being.

Donna describes how stress feels to a high Patience individual:

> Even though I feel stressed a lot of the time, I can't pinpoint an exact reason for most
> of it. My work is okay; not fantastic, but not horrible either. Things at home are okay, too.
> I have a fairly good marriage and two well-behaved kids. I take care of my elderly
> mother, and that's hard. But I don't feel like I have a right to complain, because there's no
> one else that she could live with, since my dad died last year. After his death, I have felt
> sort of numb and overwhelmed. How can I get rid of this general stressed-out feeling if
> I'm not even certain what it is that's stressing me in the first place?

We can tell that Donna is very high in Patience for a number of reasons. One is her feeling of numbness, of being overwhelmed. These emotions often go along with depression, another way of describing the submersion of feelings that Patience people do. Some people describe it as being in slow-motion—like a sense of being on hold until emotions work themselves out and can be articulated clearly and productively.

Probably Donna has not yet finished mourning for her father, even though he passed away at least a year ago. She may not have even *begun* mourning for him! This would be difficult for Dominance and Extroversion people to understand, because they tend to deal with their feelings as they arise. Put Patience people have a very deep need to process emotions internally, rather than on the surface. They won't complain or show their distress on the outside, because they don't want to upset the people around them. This means that they often carry around a terrific burden, until the time feels "right" to deal with it.

Also, Patience people may appear submissive, hesitant, and wishy-washy, going with the flow for the sake of harmony. In any group, they're the least likely to be loud, argumentative, or whiny. But they definitely have opinions, wants, and needs like everyone else. Donna may be acting unselfishly by taking care of her mother, children, husband, and duties at work. But inside, there is a secret Donna who wants to be taken care of too—who would probably love some time to herself, daily exercise, a weekend getaway, an hour every day to read or sew, or whatever it is that makes the real Donna tick. Probably if Donna had this window of personal time, it would suddenly be very clear to her why she's feeling stressed—and what she might do to feel better!

High Patience people have to understand that the world is rarely going to be as harmonious as they wish. They must become less naïve, and stop assuming that everyone shares their altruistic motives. Also, they need to give their partner permission to experience conflict and disharmonious feelings when appropriate.

To alleviate stress, Patience people crave reassurance that they are personally okay. They need a promise that the crisis will soon abate, and that progress is indeed occurring in a steady, sure manner. They want assurance in a friendly, personal way, delivered in a low-key tone that respects their need for privacy.

These needs can be taken care of by others, if they're made aware of our issues. But they can also be taken care of ourselves, with positive self-talk. Donna can give herself frequent supportive messages throughout the day, reassuring herself with the same kindness that she would give to a friend in need.

For instance, she might say to herself, "It's okay that I'm feeling stressed out right now. My dad passed away just a year ago, and everybody deserves a little slack while mourning a significant loss like this one." A statement like this validates her feelings and makes the stress seem justified and more bearable.

Or she might think as she drives home after work, "I feel overwhelmed by the duties facing me at home this evening. This is only natural, because there's plenty to be done. But I know that if I take things one at a time, the most important tasks will get accomplished. In the meantime, I know that I'm playing an important role in my relationships with the people around me, and I am truly making a difference in my own small way."

It's also important to note in discussing stress that Patience people are prone to being taken advantage of. They are not good at looking out for their own interests, and the result is often this "overwhelmed" feeling that Donna talks about. They project their behavioral motivation onto other people and are amazed when no one "takes care" of *them*. They have a hard time understanding actions that are motivated by power, money, status, or general self-interest. This makes them incredibly gullible, leading to new stressful situations.

High Patience people can reduce their stress level by learning to include themselves when they consider group or relationship needs. They can use their peacemaking talents to create peace for themselves, as well as everyone else. They should value themselves enough to provide a harmonious, pleasant environment, in which everyone has reasonable, attainable goals. Patience people need to become aware of their inner climate, just as they do so well with the social climate surrounding them. At the same time, they can give themselves little strokes, as a loving coach or mentor would, to encourage themselves and provide emotional sustenance during the day.

Stress in a large percentage of the population is caused by not having enough *patience*—and most people can actually reduce their stress by making a concerted effort to be more tolerant, laid-back, and easy-going. But the science of behavioral studies is a subtle one. The same medicine doesn't work for everyone. This explains why a high Patience person like Donna needs *less* patience. She needs to boost up a few of her other traits, like the assertiveness that goes with Dominance, or the verbal skills that go with Extroversion, to dissolve that knot of feelings inside that keeps her bound up in unexamined emotion.

Stress in Low Patience Individuals

If you're low in Patience, you feel stressed by "spinning your wheels" in your relationship, or in your life in general. It drives you crazy to wait in a long line, be delayed in traffic, or read a slow-moving book. All of these things create friction within you. People who are higher in Patience tend to irritate you, too, because they seem so slow and lethargic. "Don't they care about getting things done?" you fume to yourself. "Can't they see that the clock is ticking?"

If you review the key stressors in your relationship, and you find that many of them can be traced to low Patience ratings, then it's time to invest energy into greater self-awareness. You're never going to become more tolerant by judging yourself for being impatient. But you can become more tolerant by seeing what your impatience is doing to you and your relationships.

Maybe your low patience stress is giving you high blood pressure, pre-ulcer conditions, or constant headaches, so it's hard for you to concentrate on sex. Maybe you try to pack too much into a day, so you're always running late, causing your partner serious inconvenience. Perhaps you take your frustrations out on your loved ones, so your relationships are fraught with discord.

If you are lower in the Patience trait than your partner, evaluate whether the stress you both experience is worth the end results.

Look at the effect that your lack of Patience is having on your life, and see if it doesn't make sense to work on becoming a little more tolerant and easy-going.

How can you do that? Simply by becoming *aware* of the impatience when it steals over you. Notice the clenched jaw, or the tight fist, or whatever it is that you personally do when you get stressed. Put your attention into the jaw or fist and feel what it's like to be that part of your body at this moment. Breathe loving energy into the tight parts of your body, and tell them that it's okay. Remind yourself that there is plenty of time for everything that's really important in your day and that this moment right now is the only moment that you've ever got to be alive in. As a sage once said, "No doubt the universe is continuing on exactly as it should be," regardless of your efforts to hurry it. So reassure yourself with those calming, soothing messages you need to hear to feel relaxed and at peace.

Then give yourself the resources you need to develop good inner patience muscles. Listen to positive personal-growth tapes that teach you new self-talk skills. Find a form of meditation or prayer that suits you, and practice it every day. Do whatever it takes to get those mental gears ticking at a calm, steady pace, so you don't overheat by revving up too fast. And then be Patient by exhibiting Patience—"acting as if" you were more Patient until your inner responses conform to your new image of yourself.

Stress in High Structure Individuals

Fear is one of the primary indicators of a high Structure score. This makes sense, because in a highly structured environment, the worst thing you can do is to make a "mistake." But, as we all know, "mistakes" are very easy to make—and sometimes the people with whom we have relationships can be extremely unforgiving.

Children who grow up with very authoritative (or high Structure) parents tend to have a great deal of anxiety throughout their lives They live in constant fear of criticism. No matter how well they perform, they worry about not having the "right" house, or car, or job, or spouse, or children. They have been brought up to believe that a "right" way exists to do everything. If they fail to live up to this ideal, they expect punishment in the form of reprisals, judgment, or even eternal damnation.

So as you can see, Structure is a two-edged sword. It's of fundamental importance to an ordered society. At the same time, it creates a sense of fear, which often inhibits our freest and fullest expression as individuals. Another way of saying this is that structure creates boundaries for groups of people, but anxiety regarding these boundaries can thwart the creativity and highest potential inherent in all of us—and the potential of our interpersonal relationships.

Matt describes how stress feels when living in a High S setting:

> The greatest stress in my life is my neurotic parents. They have my whole life mapped out for me, and it sucks. They brag to their friends that they're so liberal, that they're letting me choose what I want to do in life. This translates into picking whether I want to be a doctor or a lawyer. I'm now a senior in high school, and I get to "pick" what college I'm going to, Columbia or Harvard, because that's where Dad and Uncle Saul went. If I go anywhere else, they won't pay. If I don't like it, I can go sleep under a bridge some-

where. I got my eyebrow pierced, and they said if I didn't take the ring out, they'd pull it out with pliers and make a permanent scar in my eyebrow. And if I look a little tired, they say they'll call in the police to search my room for pot. Last week I went to a movie with a girl, and when I got back they asked if I'd got herpes.

I want to strangle my parents most of the time, or move out, but I don't have any money, and they won't let me get a job because it will bring down my GPA. So how do you get people like this to shut up and realize how totally humiliating they are and leave you alone so you can grow up in peace? Don't tell me to talk to them, either. They don't listen to a word I way, because they already think they know everything in the world.

Matt's story illustrates the stress we feel when our inner self is at odds with the circumstances we find ourselves in, or when circumstances demand that we exhibit more or less of a particular behavioral trait than feels natural for us. In this case, the trait is Structure, because Matt's parents are trying to give him a set of predetermined rules to which he is expected to conform. Also, they're giving him these rules with a good deal of the Dominance trait mixed in, indicated by the fact that Matt sees little or no choice in whether to obey.

The stress that a person feels in a highly Structured relationship is created by a double-bind. You fear the consequences that are paraded in front of you should you choose not to conform. Yet you also feel a certain regret if you *do* conform, because you wonder what the other alternatives might be. There's a part in all of us that wants to do things our own way, and find our own path, regardless of how much Structure we might have in our make-up.

High Structure people naturally experience more stress than other people, because they tend to be worriers. Be patient with a worrier (even if it's yourself), but don't let excessive fear destroy your relationship.

The situation is complicated during youth and adolescence, because we don't really know who we are yet or what our unique talents might be. Only in the rarest cases does a child's genius shine forth at an early age, like a Mozart. But even Einstein failed math classes as a youngster, and Mother Teresa wasn't certain she wanted to be a nun until she was 18. Most people flourish after they've had an opportunity to be exposed to many different possibilities, so they've had a chance to find where their interests really lie. For many people, these interests change over time, as we try one avenue for a while, perhaps exhaust it or become bored with it, and then move on to something new.

The teenage years are also difficult when it comes to the Structure trait, because there are so many real dangers, which can affect us for the rest of our lives. It may sound paranoid when Matt's parents grill him about herpes, and it may embarrass him no end. But herpes and other diseases can be forever. They can be deadly. So can traffic accidents, and drug overdoses, and other things that parents worry about. Many of the Structural elements of our society are there for a very good reason, and disobedience (or non-conformity to Structure) can carry a hefty price tag.

Nevertheless, it's important to note that adolescence is a time when we want to break out of the structural molds around us. We want to try new things, flex our muscles, and find out through trial and error just who lives inside of us. Most of us make mistakes in the process. If we're lucky, we don't make too many that haunt us the rest of our lives.

If Structure issues are at the root of your relationship problems, try to determine whether they are permanent (due to inherent trait differences) or temporary (due to current circumstances). For example, if Matt is a person with a very low Structure trait who was born into a highly Structured family, then he and his parents will no doubt struggle with one another for decades to come. That's because there's a lack of shared values when it comes to the Structural expectations. If he's merely going through a normal phase at the end of high school, chafing against the worries of concerned parents, then they'll probably work through the situation sooner or later and come to a resolution when their Structural expectations are in closer alignment.

But we should not minimize the distress that Matt is experiencing now in his relationship with his parents, nor the acute distress that it's causing him. In fact, we should look at his feelings with a great deal of compassion and realize that we all find ourselves in circumstances that demand more Structure from us than we would prefer to give.

When people have more of the Structure trait than you do, they appear to be excessively precise and detailed. You view them as being perfectionists and possibly fussy. They recite a chronology of events with a litany of errors. They may seem to be unrealistically cautious and fearful, and you wonder why they can't "think outside the box."

When people have *less* of the Structure trait than you do, you may think that they're sloppy or disorganized. You may worry that they disrespect authority, which will get them into trouble. Or perhaps you feel that they aren't doing things "right." In other words, they somehow don't adhere to the same logical system that you do, and it may often grate on your nerves.

Avoid the natural tendency to judge your partner's Structure trait, regardless of whether it's higher or lower than your own. Structure differences often lead to brutal criticism, which over time can destroy even the most loving relationship.

So what do you do? If, like Matt, you're trying to deal with high Structure individuals in a relationship, you give them what they need. You also try to educate them to give you what *you* need. This reduces the stress level for everyone concerned. High Structure people need to feel safe and save face. So instead of starting World War III with them, suggest that they may be right. This relieves some of the tension right away. You praise them for their accuracy and thoroughness. You can do this regardless of whether or not you agree with them, because high Structure people are almost always both accurate and thorough.

Also, don't fly off the handle in a relationship with a high Structure individual. Stay rational, and whenever possible, present ideas in logical order, with clear reasoning. Think of incidents from the past that might prove your point—give quotes from undisputed authorities to illustrate that you're on firm factual ground. Remember that Structure people don't like being the first to do things. They distrust new ideas. They're much more comfortable if you can show that an idea has been tested, documented, and accepted by many trustworthy experts.

Another thing you should try to do is to listen to High Ss' key concerns and questions, and address them in a rational manner. Write down their objections, and then respond to them one by one. Be systematic about it. This will lessen the fears that accost them whenever they have to deal with unexpected or unorthodox suggestions.

If you're a high Structure person yourself, and you're trying to reduce your own stress level in a relationship, you can do many of the same things when talking to *yourself*. Allay your own fears by breaking them down into logical components and addressing each one in turn. Examine the possibility that there may be other ways to do things than the way they've always been done. Pat yourself on the back for your accuracy and thoroughness, and then loosen up a little bit, trusting the facts instead of checking and double-checking them. Try giving yourself some slack when it comes to perfectionism, too. You're just a person, like everyone else, and you're bound to make mistakes sooner or later. When you do, the world isn't going to come to an end. Nothing ventured, nothing gained, the old saying goes—written for people like you, who are high in the Structure trait and therefore timid about venturing into new emotional waters.

A significant shift in self-awareness occurs when we learn to distinguish where our stressful feelings are coming from—because we stop blaming them on our partner or outside circumstances. In the case of high Structure people, for instance, they can begin to realize that a great deal of their upset feelings come from that inner craving for organization and "rightness," not necessarily from the world being "wrong." The more things we can allow to be "right," the less Structure-related stress we experience. This puts us in control of our experience, rather than being victims of fate. And the more control we feel, the less stress we feel!

Stress in Low Structure Individuals

People who are low in the Structure trait face their own predictable forms of stress. Remember, these people are the risk-takers, the adventure-seekers and the trailblazers—so they feel ill at ease when forced to conform. The clear rules and hierarchical procedures that make a high Structure person comfortable will drive the low Structure person out of their mind. It is therefore important that the low Structure person determine whether conformity is an option or a necessity. If it's an option, they would do well to modify their environment. If it's a necessity, they will have to bite the bullet and modify their behavior.

For instance, suppose that a Bill, who is very low in Structure, finds himself assigned to a physics class with Miss Reubens, a very high Structure instructor. Miss Reubens insists on rigid timetables for assignments, inflexible formats for essay projects, and a very formal atmosphere in the classroom. Bill find this next to unbearable. He wants to do things at his own pace, select his own research projects, and call Miss Reubens Betty. The disparity between behavioral styles in causing a great deal of friction between the two, and Bill is in danger of failing the class. Needless to say, his stress level is high.

If the relationship with Miss Ruebens is optional, then Bill is free to change the environment, in this case by switching classes. But if she is the only physics teacher on campus, and he needs her class to finish his major, then he has no choice but to temper some of his natural Structure trait. This can be a bitter pill.

Another source of stress for low Structure people is their inability to cope with details. They're great with the big picture. But this doesn't help them when they must pay the bills on time, keep track of insurance papers, find their passport, or locate Aunt Mary's telephone number in a hurry. Because our culture is built on an assumption of Structure strengths, people who are low in the trait tend to suffer.

Take Denny as an example. Denny is a fearless yachtsman, whose daring attitude toward life demonstrates his extremely low Structure rating. But he keeps his belongings in total disarray. His "file" of personal papers consists of documents strewn amongst the socks and underwear in this bedroom bureau drawers. His airline ticket for an upcoming race may be found beneath the seat of his car, or stuffed beside the cornflakes box in the kitchen—he can never be entirely certain. He therefore wastes considerable time and money on items like duplicate documents, overdue fees at the bank and penalty charges on his income tax. He also annoys his friends, relatives and "significant other" by the general chaos in his life.

Denny is often stressed out by the inconveniences he creates for himself. But despite being in his early 60s, he has not yet realized the law of cause and effect when it comes to Structure. In other words, he does not see the inevitability of negative consequences when he cannot summon up enough Structure to meet social demands. He could reduce his stress level by complying with Structure requirements that are unavoidable (like immigration and customs forms when he enters ports of call, and proper boat registration papers), and either avoiding "optional" Structure activities or delegating responsibility for them to a trusted friend or relative.

Stamping Out "Should" Stress in Your Relationship

The Structure trait pivots around our interpretation on the word "should." People who are high in the trait are usually heavily invested in "shoulds" in life. Conversely, people who are low in the trait are often invested in not going along with the "shoulds"—or else they do not recognize that there are any "shoulds" in the first place. Being at either end of the continuum can cause stress in our relationships—either because we are trying very hard to conform to the "shoulds," or because we are trying NOT to conform to them.

In general, it's fair to say that we will be happier, more relaxed, and more effective in our relationships if we can be flexible where the "shoulds" are considered. There are many circumstances wherein it makes a lot of sense to have a healthy respect for the rules; there are also many other times when it's in our best interests to take the rules with a grain of salt. As a case in point, think of the Founding Fathers of America, who if unsuccessful during our Revolution would no doubt have been imprisoned for civil disobedience. Heroes or law-breakers? It all depends on whose set of rules you're using.

Take a good, hard look at how the Structure trait is creating stress for you and your partner, and think about how each of you might need to modify your Structure characteristics.

Managing the Stress in Your Relationship

One of the biggest reasons for becoming aware of our stress, and taking charge of it, is that it can often times be a contributor to low satisfaction in a relationship. Note the use of the word "can," rather than "is." That's because sometimes stress is actually beneficial to us. Some people can't finish a term paper without getting right up to the deadline; they thrive on the pressure that the deadline gives them. Others enjoy the adrenaline rush of a bungee jump, a fast car ride, a high-stakes poker game, or a new romantic involvement. But no one complains about this type of stress.

Negative stress, on the other hand, can cause terrible damage in our relationships, or prevent us from building healthy ones. Consider Vickie's example:

> Vickie says that her stress level is about 5, meaning that she's totally maxed out, and that she is almost a basket case because of it. The reason for her stress, she says, is that she's a total failure. She wears a size 14 now, instead of the size 8 she wore in high school. She failed the CPA test again, so she can't get the promotion at work that she wants. And she always thought that by age 27 she'd be married and own a house and have a baby, and she hasn't accomplished any of those things, even though she's already 29. Her hopelessness and overall stress level has "turned off" the few men she has dated in the past few years.

We all experience stress similar to Vickie's at some point in our lives when we fail to attain our expectations. Our attitude of disappointment creates a great deal of stress and ruins the positive ties we have established with other people in relationships. After all, no one wants a relationship with someone who is perpetually gloomy and depressed.

Where does misery like this come from? Most often from the tyranny of our own inner voices. We're all masters at making ourselves unhappy. When we aren't worrying about whether or not something awful is going to happen to us, we remember all the hurts, mistakes, and failures in the past. In other words, when we aren't preoccupied with someone or something attacking us, we turn around and attack ourselves.

Yet none of us truly lives up to expectations. We're never quite good enough, no matter how good we get. And then we keep making the same old mistakes. We suffer from guilt. We continually find fault with ourselves. We condemn ourselves constantly for not being all that we could or should be—for the broken dreams.

All this is self-hatred. We're merciless with ourselves. Then, after repeated failures and mistakes, we begin to give up on ourselves and on life. Many people, at this point, become depressed, withdrawn, and passive, accepting whatever life gives as a cruel joke that must be endured. Others, depending on their behavioral profile, turn their anger at themselves into anger at the world—or their partner. They become cranky and hostile, projecting their misery and dumping it onto other people.

Don't let self-hatred destroy the love that exists in your relationship. Take positive steps to eliminate the negative inner voices that destroy your peace of mind—so you have a more radiant self to offer your partner!

Eliminating the Stress of Self-Hatred

Here's a different way of seeing things—a new alternative that, when taken to heart, can transform your inner landscape. This is the concept that self-hatred is a state of mind: nothing more and nothing less. It's an arbitrary way of looking at life, our partner, and ourselves, and in the end it leads only to even greater misery.

One remedy is to understand how arbitrary our self-hatred is. Here's an example. Vickie is in despair because she wears a size 14 dress. But perhaps she has never considered how many women today in America would consider it a major triumph if they could fit into a size 14. Vickie thinks 14 is an embarrassingly large size. And for her, it is. But to many other people, 14 is a wonderfully small size. They'd give their eye teeth to look like Vickie.

Also, Vickie is disappointed because she had expected to be married and a mother at her age. But really, 29 is not very old at all. She still has plenty of time to meet a marriage partner and have children. In fact, anyone who is unhappily married would advise her to wait and focus more on finding a compatible partner than on the ticking biological clock.

If you have trouble believing that your self-hatred is based on *arbitrary* expectations, use another culture as a mirror. You can do this by going on a vacation to another country, reading about a foreign culture, taking a class in anthropology at your local college, watching several foreign films, or making a friend from a different country or ethnic group. You'll learn very quickly that our yardsticks for physical beauty, sociability, success, ambition, or even appropriate behavior are all determined by accidents of birth. If we had been born in a different time or place, we would expect totally different things of ourselves!

> Heather, 16, suffers from acne and is so embarrassed about her skin that she has a hard time being outgoing and friendly at school. One day, a very popular girl came up to Heather in the locker room and said how she'd give practically anything to have Heather's long, lovely legs. Heather just stood there in amazement. She'd spent months envying the other girl's beautiful complexion!

> We all want what we don't have. And we de-value that which we do have. We're all Heathers when it comes to appreciating our own talents and positive attributes.

As an exercise toward greater self-awareness, give thanks today for all of the positives in your inner savings account. When you notice those self-hate messages cropping up in your mind, gently but firmly turn them away. And in their place, plant a more constructive thought, to reinforce the new direction you want to take in life. "I am attractive, confident, and cheerful," you might repeat to yourself. "I am grateful for the opportunities that continually come my way." Refuse to give in to the old, hurtful messages of self-doubt—and even if you don't completely believe them at first, learn to feed your inner child with healing, affirming messages of hope. You'll be astounded at the changes that occur in your relationship, as you become a stronger, less stressed individual.

Is this too much to expect of ourselves? Of course not. In fact, it's the only logical way to proceed, if we truly want to explore the exciting dimensions that lie within ourselves—and relieve ourselves of the debilitating stressors that come from our own learned and arbitrary behavioral patterns.

For a better relationship, do whatever it takes to minimize the stress level you feel inside. Do your inner homework—and only then attempt to address the stress issues you experience as a couple.

Take a look at how you function in stressful situations. Ask your partner to do the same.

Exercise 7-2: Stress and You

YOU

Answer the following questions in the space provided.

How do you see your behavior under stressful situations? How do you think your partner perceives you?

How do you go from moderate stress to extreme stress? What are the physical sensations you feel your body undergoing?

What do you see happening in interactions with your partner under stressful conditions? (Do you lose your composure, patience, discipline?)

How can you deal with your partner more effectively when under stressful conditions?

YOUR PARTNER

Answer the following questions in the space provided.

How do you see your behavior under stressful situations? How do you think your partner perceives you?

How do you go from moderate stress to extreme stress? What are the physical sensations you feel your body undergoing?

What do you see happening in interactions with your partner under stressful conditions? (Do you lose your composure, patience, discipline?)

How can you deal with your partner more effectively when under stressful conditions?

Finding the cause of your stress is crucial to overcoming it. Once you pinpoint the cause of your stress, consider the following techniques for controlling it.

- Reduce fear, uncertainty, and doubt—start by identifying the major issues that bother you. Make a list of them—it might include some of the following:

  1. Primary personal relationships that aren't fulfilling
  2. A career relationship that doesn't seem to be going anywhere
  3. Lack of clarity about personal aspirations
  4. Problems with family and social relationships
  5. Poor self-esteem

- Synchronize your values and life style—understanding your values and adjusting your life style accordingly allows you to set priorities and accomplish goals.

- Write down your goals—or develop new goals for your relationship—goals that will give you a greater sense of satisfaction. Next, prioritize your goals and continually evaluate your priorities, making adjustments as appropriate. Review them several times a week to be sure you are working toward what you want.

- Avoid negative self-talk—become aware of what you think to yourself when you are under stress and turn negatives into healthy and encouraging self-talk that supports your wants.

For immediate relief the next time you are faced with a stressful situation, you could try the following quick stress relievers:

- Take four deep breaths with a seven-second inhale through the nose and an eight second exhale through the mouth.
- Shrug your shoulders one at a time, holding the pose for a few seconds and releasing, allowing the shoulders to drop as far as possible. (This will relieve stress in the neck and shoulder area.)
- Rub your temples lightly in a circular motion while concentrating on relaxing your facial muscles.
- Arch your back, tensing the muscles, hold for 10 seconds, and release.
- Make a tight fist, hold for 15 seconds, then spread your fingers wide.

Don't allow stress to take a permanent toll on your health—find the cause and treat it.

Part 8:

Appreciating and Supporting

PART EIGHT: APPRECIATING AND SUPPORTING

Introduction

Our differences are fascinating, but sometimes new and scary. Remember, you make the difference in a relationship. The most important ingredient in learning about our differences is having a sincere interest in our partner and respect for individuals in our lives who are different than we are. If you demonstrate this respect, your partner will appreciate your efforts.

Many times, some believe that "different" means "deficient" or "less valuable." Often when we look at individuals in our lives that we don't understand, we make judgments about the differences we see.

As you look at your relationship, you may be saying to yourself, "Where do I begin? So many areas need improvement. I feel completely overwhelmed." Some simple but practical suggestions are provided below that you can put to work right away for almost immediate results. Hopefully, these results will give you the necessary strength to tackle and conquer most of the problems facing your relationship.

It is up to you to overcome any pet peeves or barriers that can infect a relationship. A pet peeve is an emotional hot button that causes you to have a quick, strong reaction to a word, a behavior, or mannerism.

Identify several of your personal pet peeves. Also, indicate how you react to a partner with a behavior you find irritating.

My Pet Peeves	**How I respond to them?**
_____	_____
_____	_____
_____	_____
_____	_____
_____	_____
_____	_____

Being aware of your personal preferences is essential in a relationship. But also, notice that a behavior you find distracting, bothersome, or irritating may be just fine or even desirable to your partner. Monitor your responses. Remember, most behaviors are learned, and acceptable behavior varies from person to person.

We are often most comfortable with individuals whom we perceive to be like ourselves. This explains why we show only our best side during the courting phase. Then after awhile, the relationship becomes more complex, and we begin to notice irritants. We relax and become more true to ourselves.

You can control your own attitude, feelings, and comfort level, and develop the knowledge and skill to handle irritating moments. Behaviors and skills can be learned and practiced daily.

Exercise 8-1: Evaluate How You Are Doing

Think of a problem that came up recently between you and your partner.

What was the situation?

Were you able to anticipate your partner's needs or expectations?

Were you successful in resolving the conflict?

What would you do differently in the future?

Identify two problem areas in your relationship.

Problem One:

Ideas for resolving the conflict.

Problem Two:

Ideas for resolving the conflict.

A lack of sensitivity to the behavior or communication style of your partner may cause you to be blind to your own behavior. Insensitive people tend to see only a behavior in their partner that is markedly different from their own.

The following exercise is designed to pinpoint the areas where you might be insensitive to your partner's needs or desires.

Exercise 8-2: What I Do That Drives My Partner Up the Wall

List the things you do that drive your partner crazy.

(Examples: Completing his sentences for him. Eating while she talks to me on the phone. Speeding through amber traffic lights.)

Why do you think these behaviors are so irritating? What thoughts came to your mind?

(Examples: He wants to explain his own ideas. She's hypoglycemic and needs an immediate snack. He thinks it's uncool to slow down at an intersection.)

Did you have any feelings of anger?

What did you learn about yourself in relationship to your partner?

Taking Personal Responsibility

To take personal responsibility requires the maturity to actively "own" and express our thoughts, feelings, needs, and intuitions in a way that shows we understand how we've co-created a particular situation. We're willing to hold ourselves accountable for our own "side of the street." We are keenly aware of our personal integrity, as distinct from others. We tend to use "I" statements instead of "You" statements.

An "I" statement looks like this:

- "I feel really furious right now, " instead of "You're such a jerk."
- An "I" statement communicates how you experience your partner's behavior.
- An "I" statement is feedback, not criticism. It lets your partner know how his or her behavior affects you.
- An "I" statement is usually experienced as a positive attempt to communicate your needs and concerns. Therefore, your partner is more likely to respond effectively than if he or she were coerced into doing so.

"I" Statements Worksheet

- Describe a behavior in your partner that you find unacceptable.
- Describe the feelings you have about the behavior.
- Describe how the behavior affects you in any tangible way.

Example: Your partner continually interrupts you both in public and privately. Up to now, you have silently endured it. "You" statement would be: "You are so rude I can't believe it!"

Example: "I" Statement Formula

Description of Behavior	Feelings	Effects on Me
Interrupting when I'm talking	Hurt, frustrated, put down, embarrassed	Can't say what I want

"I" Statement: "I get frustrated when you interrupt me because I can't finish what I want to say."

I urge you to experiment with using "I" statements. The only way to accurately assess their impact is to use them.

You can change yourself, but you can't change others.

We have all heard this many times, but it really does bear remembering: *we cannot change others*. We only have the ability to change ourselves. For others to feel safe with us, we must consistently be willing to keep the focus on our own emotional turf. We can use statements such as, "I must have misunderstood, I'm sorry" rather than, "You misled me." But this works only if we mean it. If we aren't sincere, our tone of voice and body language will betray our real feelings.

To trust, to feel connected in the relationship, and to feel heard, your partner must have some way of comprehending that you are being supportive. You must communicate your support in ways that your partner will understand. (Refer to the section on communication by behavioral type, Part Six).

To know your partner is receiving your communication, watch for clues. These range from shifts in body language (posture, arm position, breathing) and gestures (large to small, small to large), to changes in facial features—skin color, mouth, eyes, jaw movements, shifts in voice (tone, rhythm, value, tempo) or shifts in language patterns (types of words, length of sentences).

When you notice a shift, you know that something different has happened. This may be positive or negative. Many of us have a long history of blaming the other person for not understanding us. We should each take responsibility for being understood. Continually check the "connection" to make sure your partner is with you.

When you and your partner don't deal with uncomfortable issues between you, the problems don't go away. They gradually smolder and can create a serious break in rapport. This is the opposite of what you want—remember, you are working toward creating a "connection."

> Jim is a very outgoing High E, and he enjoys flirting with women wherever he goes. His wife, Judy, is a very Low E, and she feels devalued and threatened by his behavior. After 20 years of marriage, the issue has eaten away at her self-esteem so badly that she feels undesirable in bed and turns a cold shoulder when Jim tries to initiate sex. The issue is such a deep and disturbing one that she has never even considered discussing it with Jim.

How many times have you and your partner been in a conversation and then something happens that creates discomfort? Did you address it?

A common mistake one often makes in giving tough messages in a relationship is to put up smoke screens in order to avoid issues you fear will be painful. This is most common in Low Ds and High Ps. Avoiding a difficult situation, however, often makes it worse. In general, the harder a situation is to communicate, the more important it is to be direct and show respect.

Clarify the problem and define your view, then focus on the *problem* rather than the *person*. If you are in a position to receive a tough message—then **listen**. When you take responsibility to mention that you've noticed a problem, then there is a chance to resolve the problem and move forward.

Become Best Friends

Have you ever noticed that people sometimes treat perfect strangers with more courtesy and kindness than they do their own partners? If a relationship is to have any measure of success or happiness, you must be committed to treating your partner with respect, dignity, and love. In short, act as though your partner is your best friend—one you would never risk losing. The key word here is *act*—because if you do not translate your attitude into actions, your relationship can wither.

Each friend represents a world in us, a world possibly not born until they arrive, and it is only by this meeting that a new world is born.

- Anais Nin

When two people decide to live together as best friends, they complement each other, with each person finding a greater wholeness in the partnership. To be a whole is a challenge. Living together demands understanding each other's behaviors, attitudes, expectations, and habits. Living together well is an art that requires paying attention to a great many details at once and being able to do the same thing over and over again each day. When things go wrong, you must immediately right the wrong, whatever the personal sacrifice, and start over again, accepting each other. Learn to grow with moving—from the comfortable to the uncomfortable and back again. The better things go today, the more chance for pleasure and harmony tomorrow.

Exercise 8-3

Occasionally, it is important to remind ourselves why we have chosen to spend our lives with our partners. This exercise can help.

Choose a time when you both will be uninterrupted for at least 20 minutes. Sit facing each other and take turns completing this sentence, "You are my best friend because . . ." Your sentences can be serious, such as, "You are my best friend because you can always help me find the best in any situation." Or they can be lighthearted, such as, "You are my best friend because you laugh at my bad puns—even when you've heard them before!" By telling your partner why you like him or her, and by listening to why your partner likes you, you will reconnect with the foundation upon which your loving relationship is built.

Believe in Each Other

A common thread in all effective relationships is the caring attention the partners give each other. Lovers truly love to be together. They believe in each other and are proud of each other. The experiences of life and the real world can keep your partner down and discouraged unless an opposing force of love and support is always there. You can demonstrate your belief in your partner by taking the following actions:

- **Speak well of your partner**. One way to demonstrate your belief in each other is to speak well of your partner and to respond with good words even if your partner's speech becomes harsh, critical, or insulting. You decide to bless your partner by the words you speak. This can require significant amounts of the Patience trait, if you're starting to feel annoyed, or the Extroversion trait if it's hard for you to express your feelings. "You were the most attractive woman in the whole room to me tonight."—music to any woman's ears, especially if it's heart-felt.

- **Do kind things for your partner**. Solve irritating relationship problems with kindness and understanding rather than criticism and selfishness. For example, if your partner repeatedly leaves the cap off the toothpaste, simply put the cap on yourself—with a smile. This will allow you to save your energy for building up the relationship, rather than tearing it down. If you leave the cap off the toothpaste and it bothers your partner, consider changing this habit. You might even try compromising and purchasing two tubes of toothpaste, one for each of you. You have the choice of deciding whether to make this an issue worthy of battle. The point is to do something kind and pleasing for your mate—not as a duty, but as a gift of love. Try to do this every day.

**Enhance caring
behavior with
unanticipated
pleasures.**

- **Show thankfulness and appreciation for who your partner is**. Whatever you can find to appreciate in your partner, make it known verbally—not just to your mate, but to other significant people in your lives as well. "I really appreciate having a solid, reliable husband like you. I wouldn't trade you for any other man in the world."

- **Want the very best for your partner in all circumstances**. Don't fall into the trap of competing with your spouse, even if you are pursuing the same or similar careers. Let their victories be yours. "Go for it when you run that marathon, and I'll be cheering for you every step of the way!"

Build Each Other Up

"Make thy love larger to enlarge my worth," Elizabeth Barrett Browning wrote to the man she would marry. When you build your partner up, your love for each other grows, because the self-worth of the beloved is nourished. This is a greatest gift you can give your partner.

Look for beauty within another spirit.

Love always builds up, never tears down. This gives your partner freedom to grow and develop as a person without fear of failure or hurtful criticism. Some partners learn how to refrain from criticism but do not complete the "building up" cycle by learning the art of praise. It has been said, "The best way to compliment your spouse is frequently." Relationships can simply dry up because of what you do not say.

Here are nine ways you can encourage and build up your partner. This list is not comprehensive, and I encourage you to add to it as you grow in your relationship.

- Make the irrevocable decision never again to be critical of your partner in thought, word, or deed. This may sound like an impossibility, but is not. It is simply a decision backed by action until it becomes a habit you could not change if you wanted to.

- Study your partner. Become sensitive to the areas where your partner feels a lack and think of ways to build them up. Self-confidence is a key factor to anyone's success. As a partner, you hold great power in your ability to help bolster your loved one's self-confidence. Provide lots of praise for the partner's hard work, good intentions, and attempts toward personal growth. Such praise creates the energy that encourages continued hard work and enthusiasm.

- Be accepting. One of the secrets to happiness in any relationship is accepting others as they are. Don't try to change your partner into someone else. Think back to when you first met. Remember what you saw that was worthwhile and appealing. Remember you only have the power to change yourself. So if you are seeking change, begin there.

- Think every day of the positive qualities and behavior patterns you admire and appreciate in your mate. Refuse to entertain any critical observations so they have no chance of rooting in your mind.

- Consistently verbalize praise, and show appreciation for your partner. Be genuine, be specific, be generous. Thoughts have no impact unless they are spoken.

- Recognize your partner's talents, abilities, and accomplishments. Communicate your respect for the work your partner does.

- Demonstrate how much your partner means to you publically and privately. Be sparing in your admiration of other people of the same sex as your partner. This rarely, if ever, has a positive effect on a relationship. Instead, keep your attention focused on your partner.

Studies on millions of men indicate that the most attractive attribute in a woman is not her figure, hair or legs, but her *smile*.

- Show your partner that he or she is the most important person in your life. Seek each other's opinions and value each other's judgments. Pay close attention to everything the partner says and does.

- Respond to each other physically and facially. The face is your most distinctive and expressive communication tool. Your partner wants to see you smile, with eyes sparkling in response.

- Always show the greatest courtesy to each other. You should both be VIPs in your own home.

- Guard and appreciate the precious time you have together, as if it is your greatest treasure. (It is!)

- Write a list of specific ways in which you can encourage and build up your partner.

Real communication—
real "supporting"—
real "appreciating"—
is reaching out to your partner,
understanding them,
walking in their shoes,
sharing their dreams and fears,
and celebrating their gifts.

Part 9:

*Healing
Relationships*

Part Nine: Healing Relationships

Introduction

What gives people happiness in their everyday lives is the ability to form and maintain strong, positive relationships. The basis for most relationships is one's getting what one wants from another person and, in return, giving something back. We want another's goodwill and friendship. We want acceptance and recognition.

In a relationship, how you relate has a direct effect on how that person relates to you. Put another way, what you give is what you get.

Myriad situations arise between two people in a relationship. Some are heartbreaking; some are perplexing and unbelievably complicated; but very few are truly hopeless. Although it is not possible in this book to address the entire breadth of issues that arise in a relationship, the following is a careful attempt to look at some of the more important elements of success.

> **Those who bring sunshine into the lives of others cannot keep it from themselves.**
>
> – J. M. Barrie

One of the first steps in making constructive changes in any area of your life is to face the issues honestly. Diagnose your relationship to assess where you are in your relationship versus where you would like to be. Considering which of the following statements best describes your situation may help you with your self-diagnosis. Put a check mark next to any statements that fit.

___ • We have a good relationship now, but we want an even better one.

___ • We have never had a healthy relationship.

___ • We have lost the spark that we once felt together.

___ • Frankly, I am no longer in love with my partner.

___ • My partner seems indifferent and doesn't seem to care.

___ • We care about each other, but our relationship is dull.

___ • I want to restore and save the relationship, but my partner is uncooperative.

__ • My partner wants to split up.

__ • We have serious problems, but we agreed on trying to save our relationship.

__ • Both of us want to learn how to make this a healthy, fulfilling relationship.

__ • We're new in this relationship, and we want to build something that will last and become more enjoyable all the time.

Be encouraged about the future of your relationship. The relationship you would like to have with your partner *can happen*, but not by accident. A relationship seldom improves spontaneously.

> **The greatest thing in the world is not so much where we stand as in which direction we are moving.**
> - Oliver Wendell Holmes

But if you make a decision to learn everything you can about a fulfilling relationship and put the things you learn into practice, your relationship will blossom. If your relationship is already strong, it will become even better!

At any stage in the relationship, even if you've been wavering on the edge of a traumatic separation, your relationship can usually be rekindled, if this is what both of you want. You can learn to deal with even the most difficult problems in such a way that your relationship will become rooted—stabilized and strong enough to hold up through the stresses of a lifetime.

- To build a healthy, fulfilling relationship, you need to recognize a unique value in your partner and choose to affirm that value always. Love is a choice that is backed by action.

- Developing a relationship is an art that you must want to learn and pour yourself into. The key to a harmonious life with your partner lies in accommodating what your partner would like you to be—and simultaneously being the person *you* were meant to be. What does each partner want, need, and desire from the relationship? What is each partner looking for in a relationship?

- You are not a helpless slave or victim in a relationship. It is important to grasp this principle and realize that a relationship doesn't "just happen," as it is often depicted in movies. The truth is, a relationship has only the power that you give it with your own free will. *You* have the power to rekindle, restore or abandon the relationship, and you can refuse to be trapped in less-than-satisfactory conditions.

- Radiate love and happiness instead of trying to attract these characteristics in a mate. The media tends to depict a healthy relationship as only being available to those who are physically desirable—if you use the proper toothpaste, perfume, shaving cream, shampoo, deodorant, and so on. The true secret of being lovable, however, has nothing to do with products. The secret is learning to *give* love rather than obtaining it from someone else.

> Recognize that you are the author of your choices, actions, and fulfillment. No one else can make you truly happy or give you self-esteem.

Most of us have one person in our life who matters a great deal to us, but we aren't comfortable with each other and the relationship is strained and suffering. This might be your partner, parent, former friend, or neighbor. Often these broken relationships cause us a great deal of pain, regret, and guilt, and we would give almost anything to have them restored.

Here are some secrets for healing a broken relationship:

- **Do something together—just the two of you**. By experiencing an activity one-on-one, you will be forced to rely on each other for help, wisdom, and expertise. Take a trip, do a jigsaw puzzle, go out for lunch, or simply take a walk. You will start listening to each other in new ways. You will start to recognize the old, automatic reactions for what they are—offensive maneuvers that weren't getting the two of you anywhere.

- **Apologize**. "I'm sorry," ought to be a very easy thing for you to say. Apologize even when you're not 100% certain you were at fault. The benefits of repairing the relationship almost always outweigh any damaged pride you might suffer.

> Intensify your emotional bond with high-energy fun.

- **Be open to changing how you feel and think**. Don't spend all of your time trying to make the other person see things your way. Instead, think about how you might behave differently, so the other person will see you from a new perspective.

- **Be willing to forgive**. If you want to move on emotionally, you must forgive old hurts. Until then, you will be giving the other person power over you. When you forgive someone, you not only free that person, but you free yourself as well. Force yourself to *prove* your forgiveness through actions. Write a friendly note. Demonstrate in some very clear manner that you're not holding a grudge.

- **Accept that the other person probably means well**. It's important to realize that when people act in a thoughtless way, they probably had valid reasons for doing so. Very rarely will anyone intentionally hurt your feelings. So give others the benefit of the doubt.

- **Don't try to control the other person's feelings**. You can't change what another person thinks, believes, or does, You can only take control of your side of the relationship. Being responsible for your own behavior is often enough to encourage the other person to begin changing.

- **Don't take everything personally**. When another person does something that bothers you, ask if the behavior is really directed at you. It usually isn't. Realizing this allows you to avoid unnecessary conflict.

- **Make an effort to be yourself**. Think about how you change when you are with another person. Try hard to stay out of roles and be genuine.

- **Let the other person know what you admire about him or her**. This can be very difficult if you are angry. Nevertheless, your acceptance of others as being great people in some ways—often in many ways—sets you free from the need to rebel against them or find fault.

- **Pay individual attention to the special people in your life**. The most common complaint of partners in a relationship is that they're taken for granted. Don't let it happen in yours.

Evaluate Your Relationship

Ask yourself probing questions that—when answered honestly—give you insight into how you currently set priorities in strengthening and healing your relationship.

- Am I critical of my partner? How? (Be specific.)
- Do I expect my partner to be perfect, or do I allow for individual differences?
- Am I willing to give my partner something in return for something I want?
- Do I cut my partner down in order to enhance my own self-esteem?
- Do I give my partner enough attention? Am I genuinely interested in my partner's problems?
- Do I accept my partner as an equal?
- Do I have respect for my partner's individuality?
- Do I treat my partner as considerately as I would like to be treated?
- Am I a good communicator? Am I easy to be around?
- Do I listen attentively, and frequently enough, to my partner?
- Am I skillful in getting my thoughts, ideas, and feelings across to my partner?
- When I ask my partner to help, do I allow him or her to participate? Do I share the benefits?
- Do I praise my partner? How long has it been since I gave a real compliment?
- Am I sincere with my partner?
- Am I too impatient with my partner?
- Am I holding grudges?
- Does my temper get me in trouble with my partner?

Given your answers to the exercise, list some steps you would like to take to improve your relationship:

Choosing Better Relationships

Many of the most important relationships in our lives are already fixed. We can't get new parents. We have no control over which children are born to us. And we're reluctant to change spouses unless things are very bad and there is no hope of improvement.

But there are other times when we can use our knowledge of behavioral traits to make better choices in partners from the outset. When dating, we want to make wise selections. For a business partner, we want to ensure long-term compatibility.

In the following story, notice how Gretel's long-term goals will determine her choice in a mate:

Gretel, the owner of a thriving real estate agency, has an enviable dilemma on her hands. Two very eligible bachelors have proposed to her, and she can't decide between them. She loves each one in a different way, and she can see two tempting but very different futures ahead of her, depending on her choice. She has therefore turned to behavioral analysis profiles for help in making up her mind.

First, let's take a look at Gretel's profile, so we know what she might be expecting in lifetime partner. Her strongest trait is Dominance (D), followed by a much lower but still significant Structure (S) factor. This means that she likes to have things her way and she tends to play life "by the rules." She cares a great deal about details—she dots every "i" and crosses every "t," a valuable habit in her profession. She also enjoys being in control, which has made her an effective manager and entrepreneur.

Her low traits are Extroversion and Patience. From this we know that she tends to be shy around new people, conservative in outlook, uncomfortable with large social groups, and rather impulsive in decision-making. When she goes to annual real estate conventions, for instance, she tends to spend time with one or two close friends, and walks out of seminars as soon as her interest wanes.

Sean, one of Gretel's suitors, is also highest in Dominance, but at the same time he is an Extrovert and a nonconformist. He runs a rival real estate office across town, and he and Gretel maintain a fiercely competitive business relationship. Yet they have a lot of fun together during their off hours since Sean always thinks of exciting things to do. On Gretel's birthday, he surprised her with a getaway weekend in Las Vegas. On Valentine's Day, he hired a country-western band to play in her office parking lot all afternoon. When Gretel describes Sean to her friends, she says that he makes her heart pound faster.

The funny thing about Sean is that while his flashiness and popularity appeal very strongly to Gretel, they also worry her. She wonders whether the extravagance that seems so romantic during courtship might feel wasteful after they have been married a while. What if she tires of the groups of people Sean always surrounds himself with? How will she handle his lack of conventionality when it comes to something she feels very strongly about, such as religious training for children they might one day have?

But on the other hand, there's the financial set-up to think about. Like many people high in Dominance, Sean and Gretel both make a lot of money. They both are driven to excel and they value the bottom line. No doubt they will prosper as a couple even more than they do today on their own, which is a big point in Sean's favor.

One consideration Gretel should also be weighing is the flip side to the Dominance trait she and Sean share. People with High D need to win. While Gretel and Sean might enjoy mutual competition in a business setting, it will almost inevitably lead to difficulties in a marriage. Neither one can win all the time at home. And their secondary traits are so diametrically opposed that they will probably end up butting heads on issue after issue because they have such divergent needs for social interaction and compliance.

Peter, Gretel's other suitor, is at the other end of the behavioral spectrum. He's a professional flutist with the city symphony and a committed environmentalist. He is happiest when practicing a Vivaldi concerto alone hour after hour or hiking in the back country whenever he can get out of town. His highest trait is Patience, followed by Structure, and his lowest trait is Extroversion.

Gretel finds herself feeling very serene and centered around Peter, exactly the opposite of the adrenaline rush she gets around Sean. On dates, she and Peter dine in quiet restaurants by candlelight or sit beside an alpine lake far from the sounds of the freeway. They read side by side. When she feels strongly about something, Peter gives in to her wishes, preferring harmony over making a fuss.

But fusses are rare, because Peter and Gretel usually agree on things. They come from similar educational and family backgrounds and they both take for granted that certain rules in life will be followed. They change the oil in their cars within days of receiving a reminder from the gas station. They pay their bills on time. They meticulously follow the cleaning directions on clothing labels.

The similarities between Gretel and Peter's low Extroversion and high Structure traits could be viewed either positively or negatively, depending on what each person wants in a partnership. Two introverts can certainly enjoy the intimacy of being alone together, but they can also become isolated from the rest of the world if they don't make an effort to socialize. Two conformists can live together very happily once they agree on which set of rules to follow. But they can also get stuck in their ways, and life can become boring unless they consciously strive to add a little adventure and spontaneity.

Gretel's strong Dominance trait and Peter's lack of Dominance can swing either way as well. The fact that Peter lets Gretel make all the decisions means that they have few arguments. But then Gretel sometimes feels uncomfortable "wearing the pants," as her mother puts it, especially in public when Peter refuses to take the lead. Peter, for his part, has become less assertive as the relationship has evolved, and Gretel fears that over time he might just fade into the woodwork. She also worries about what will happen as her business continues to prosper and she vastly out-earns Peter, who lacks the ambition or interest in financial success to budge from his comfortable (but not highly paid) chair with the orchestra.

The choice between Sean and Peter will not be an easy one for Gretel, because there is no right or wrong answer. Each man offers her a different growth path with distinct merits and potential pitfalls. Does she want to develop her Dominance and tone down her Structure? Then she should join Sean in the fast lane. Would she rather nurture her Patience, sustain her Structure, and consider working on softening her Dominance? Then Peter is the better choice.

Even to make her decision, however, she must take a step back from her own Structure trait and understand that it's okay to take a risk. She can probably build a happy marriage with either man, but they will be very different kinds of marriages. And depending on which man she picks, she will find herself maturing into a very different person as the years go by, and as she and either Sean or Peter make the inevitable behavioral adjustments that a successful marriage requires.

Have you selected relationships that are for your highest good? Do you feel trapped in your current relationship, or do you see opportunities for limitless growth?

There are no right or wrong answers to these questions. Also, your response will most likely change from one day to the next, depending on your mood.

> **Recognize that your own intuition is a valuable and valid source of information and guidance.**

Use all of the information in this book to make better long-term commitments and to improve the committed relationships you already have.

Part 10:

Creating
Fulfillment

PART TEN: CREATING FULFILLMENT

Introduction

By this time, you have many new insights into yourself that you can use as a foundation for change. You also have many ideas and tools to work with as you move toward a life filled with excitement, challenges, and satisfaction.

Many of us have had mentors and teachers along the way that have had great impact on us, whether it be by something they said, something they did, or just by their very presence. Don't pass up opportunities to learn from other people's experiences.

As we imperceptibly become more aware of ourselves, we experience moments in our lives that we identify as turning points—places where our world and our sense of self become larger. Not that we jump out of our chairs and shout "Eureka!" at the sudden emergence of our true selves. Nor are we different people on Wednesday than we were on Tuesday. But some moments leap out from the ordinary because they sustain our sense of what is possible.

To maintain and grow any relationship, we must be willing to risk, challenge, and be vulnerable to a degree.

Such moments can take place in a relationship. When one partner opens up to another, there are moments that are often undefinable to their depth. Maintaining a fulfilling relationship is often challenging at best, for we all bring to it our own "story"—we all come from different backgrounds, have different ways of doing things, and have different values, likes, and dislikes. But if we view all those differences with respect, we will be able to see the gift in each individual.

Willingness to risk, challenge, and be vulnerable to a degree in any relationship is necessary not only for the maintenance of the relationship, but for growth as well. It is also important to be willing to look at one's self in the process. Taking responsibility for ourselves and respecting the diversity in our partner will serve us well in the pursuit and enhancement of our relationship.

Become Passionate

Many people tend to join the "rat race," or even totally withdraw for some years, but somehow they seem to plunge back into some new adventure, reviving themselves and starting life anew. What is it that drives these people to lift themselves up and start living once again?

In many cases, this newly-found energy can be attributed to *passion*. A new interest, a desire to improve a relationship can spark *passion* that can propel people further than they have ever dreamed. With *passion* comes confidence and a desire to explore the very depths of what you are so drawn to. You must first be open to the possibility of becoming passionate about your relationship, for it can be somewhat risky—you may take chances you wouldn't ordinarily take if you weren't passionate!

Be open to the possibilities of passion. It can give you new vitality and excitement that is so necessary in everyone's life today.

Revitalizing Your Relationship

As we become more aware of ourselves, we come to turning points - places where our world and our sense of self become larger. Not that we jump out of our chairs and shout "Eureka!" at the sudden emergence of our true selves. Nor are we different people on Wednesday than we were on Tuesday. But we do have times where insights startle us into growth, because they create a new sense of what is possible.

> **The key to maintaining a healthy, meaningful relationship lies in nurturing mutual personal growth.**

Such moments can take place in a relationship. When one partner opens up to another, you discover new facets to explore together. You see hints of new emotional depths. And when *both* of you open up, the growth potential is astronomical.

Where does renewed intensity and richness come from in a relationship? From the willingness to risk. We move out of our inner comfort zones. We trust a little more than we did yesterday. We ask the unexpected question, or show interest in an area that we've always taken for granted. Or perhaps we introduce an element of the unknown. Regardless of the means selected, we find a way to bring back some of that excitement that drew us together in the first place.

S.O.S. for Relationships on the Rocks

If it feels like your relationship has run aground lately, and you're worried that things are starting to fall apart, consider these three steps for rescuing a floundering relationship. First, pull up the anchors. Then clear the decks. Finally, fill your sails. Here's how:

1. **Pull Up the Anchors.** Figure out what's stopping the two of you from moving forward together. Is it that you've become bored with one another? Are you both burned out by high-stress careers? Are the demands of children taking away the time you used to spend one-on-one? Or are there deeper problems beneath the surface, which need addressing?

   Your primary task in "pulling up the anchors" of your relationship is to determine what the anchors are, and get to work dislodging them. Maybe you need to go see a counselor or other trained professional, for help in articulating your concerns. Perhaps a drug or alcohol problem is serving as the anchor, holding back interpersonal growth.

   Along with anchors, you might each have a lot of extra ballast that you're bringing into the relationship, making it difficult to get off the rocks. Examples might be hostility toward a parent that is projected onto your mate. Or there may be unresolved issues from a prior romantic attachment. How much longer do you plan to haul these negative attitudes around in your life? Toss them overboard - and experience that wonderful sense of freedom that comes from letting go!

   One of the most dangerous anchors in a relationship is an unforgiven hurt. An affair that's over but not forgotten. An unkind comment that permanently damaged your partner's self-esteem. An open wound in your heart, resulting from a slight, misunderstanding or argument.

If either of you hangs on to unforgiven hurts, you can count on staying anchored to the rocks. Take a good, hard look at your internal landscape - because that's how it's going to stay for a very long time. In fact, things are only going to get worse. Unless both of you are willing to budge, the hurt is never going to go away, and your relationship will sour and die.

Differences in each of the four behavioral traits create predictable rocks for a relationship. Your particular behavioral trait differences have not *caused* the lack of magic in your relationship, but they have certainly contributed to its demise. Go back to your SAS reports, and notice where especially large trait differences might create shoals. Are these the places where you are currently stuck? Can you see where each of you will need to push either up or down on your various traits?

Check out the Dominance differences between the two of you. Dominance can be a tricky issue in a relationship, especially if both of you want to be in charge. Both people usually arrive at a compromise early on, sometimes spoken and sometimes not. The compromise can divide up control in any number of ways. "I'm the boss in the kitchen, and you're the boss of the garage." "You decide everything, and I'll just go along with whatever you want." "We'll live fairly independent lives, and take turns making major decisions."

But even with a compromise in place, every relationship will run into Dominance-related complications. You can head many of these off before they occur by doing preventive maintenance on your behavior. If you're higher than your partner in Dominance, then let them have their own way. (You may have to coax their wishes out of them, as they might have grown unaccustomed to thinking for themselves.) If you're lower in D than your partner, then get a little more assertive. Instead of meeting resistance, you may find your mate pleasantly surprised by your show of character.

Extroversion differences can stall otherwise good relationships, too. You may prefer intimate dinners at home, while your partner wants to have big parties. They may enjoy silently holding hands before a sunset, while you want to tell a long story or expound on the poetry of the sun's last rays.

If your Extroversion rating is higher than your partner's, then force yourself to be a listener more often. Ask questions that prove that you're paying attention. Try to draw out your partner, and be sensitive to their unspoken messages. For the more introverted partner, work hard to verbalize your thoughts and emotions. Butt into the conversation more frequently, even at the risk of feeling impolite. The health of your relationship could depend on it!

Patience trait differences can be problematic, but are typically not as dangerous as Dominance or Structure issues. For the partner with the most Patience, beware of internalizing conflict. Learn to trust your loved ones by sharing your feelings, and don't always put their needs before your own. If you do, you will end up exhausted and spent, and you'll wonder where your real self went. The partner with the lower Patience score needs to slow down your emotional engine, and become more tolerant of others' needs. Try to notice what your partner wants before they tell you, and offer them the same type of selfless service that they give to you.

Structure can be a difficult trait to reconcile, since it triggers deep fears in people, and affects their overall comfort level in the relationship. So if you notice Structure-type issues on the horizon, take action. Ask yourself whether you are willing to be flexible when it comes to Structure. Could you tolerate a slightly messier closet? Would it be okay to balance the checkbook once a week instead of after every transaction?

If you are high in Structure, and it's creating an anchor between the two of you, try to figure out just how important the issue is—and whether you're willing to budge. If you subscribe to a particular set of religious practices and your fiancee does not, then decide which is a priority to you, the practices or the relationship. If you and your husband always quarrel over wet towels on the bathroom floor, then evaluate whether tidiness is worth the nagging.

The partner with the lower Structure score needs to be sensitive, too, in avoiding trouble before it happens. Could you sacrifice a little to give your partner the order they require? Or is their fearfulness so great that you find it dampens your natural spontaneity? Weigh the options carefully, understanding that your partner will tend to "hear" criticism if you bring up the subject incorrectly.

"Let there be spaces in your togetherness, And let the winds of the heavens dance between you. Love one another, but make not a bond of love. Let it rather be a moving sea between the shores of your souls."
– Kahlil Gibran, The Prophet

2. **Clear the Decks.** After you have located the anchors in your relationship, and pulled them up to the best of your ability, then it's time to clear the decks. This means creating space in your relationship for surprises, growth and fun.

Remember when the two of you were just getting to know each other? You set aside your best hours to be together. You made certain that distractions could not interrupt your intimacy. You made dates, went on weekend trips, saved special times for one another. In short, you created a sacred space in the middle of your individual lives, which you kept swept clean of extraneous concerns, so that your relationship could deepen. And you guarded this private time as your most treasured asset.

What are the decks like now in your relationship? Are they littered with sacks of obligations and piles of old garbage, so there's no room to dance and play? Have the decks become pitted through lack of maintenance? Is the general appearance ship-shape, so you're prepared for exciting voyages together.

Stow those bulky distractions in the hold of your ship. Swab down all of the surfaces on your decks, until they gleam in the sunshine and practically beg for adventure. Make your togetherness so inviting, in fact, that both of you treasure it more than anything else in your lives. You'll know when this task is accomplished by the fact that you start to become irresistible to one another again - and you begin contemplating the next step - revitalizing the magic between you.

3. **Fill the Sails.** Now you're ready for the real fun in life—raising the sails in your relationship, catching the wind in them, and seeing where the Universe will carry you. Will the breezes puff gently, or will they blow you to unexpected ports of call? Will it be smooth sailing, or will you run into hurricanes and heavy seas? There's no telling. But whatever you encounter, the two of you will be together, facing the forces of nature together, and being the very best crewmates as possible.

    Your job at this point is to keep the sails filled. Trim the jib and keep your boat in tip-top condition. The following basic principles will help:

    Reach out and touch. Remember all those things that made you so excited when the two of you first started a relationship? The way the merest brush of his hand could make you tremble? The way her fingers on the back of your neck could set your whole body tingling? Our bodies need constant reminders of affection, and when we don't get them, part of our hearts shut down as well. So reach your foot under the table and give him a secret reminder that you care. Give her a shoulder rub when she least expects it. When you sense that there's distance growing between the two of you, then give an extra hug—for no reason at all. You'll be amazed at home physical contact can often communication much more than words ever could, and heal the most strained feelings between two people.

> Happiness in marriage consists of falling in love over and over again with the same person.
> –Rev. Dale Turner, Seattle Times

Practice praise. Give your loved one compliments all throughout the day, and watch how their face lights up. There's a great deal of wisdom in the old saying, "If you can't say something nice, then don't say anything at all." Often when we've been in a relationship for some time, we forget to consider whether our comments are kind. We just say whatever pops into our minds, and this can be very damaging to the self-esteem of the other person. An added benefit you'll receive when you begin saying nicer things to someone is that you'll start thinking nicer things too. This helps to realign your mental state on a more positive frequency, bringing improvements in healthy, energy and general well-being.

Be generous with affection. Tell your wife that there's no other woman in the world that you'd rather be married to. Tell your son that you're proud to be his parent. Act like a magnanimous millionaire with your affectionate remarks, and don't be afraid to put your feelings into words. Practice in front of the mirror if you have to, until speaking affectionately comes as easily as breathing. The right comment at the right time will be treasured by the listener forever.

Start the day with love. Greet your partner with a smile and a cheery "good morning." Create new possibilities for intimacy early in the morning, if the two of you feel so inclined. Don't leave the bed until the two of you have re-established your bond together, even it's only with a caress on the cheek.

Never go to bed angry with one another. While it may be difficult to resolve an issue late at night, and you may be too tired to resolve it to your complete satisfaction, you must still try to reach some sort of compromise so that neither party feels wounded. Going to sleep while you're mad releases damaging toxins into your body; besides, you won't sleep well anyway. It's much better to take whatever time is necessary to come to a conclusion—even if the conclusion is that you agree to table the issue until tomorrow, and give each other a kiss in the meantime.

Behave with uncommon courtesy. Don't kid yourself into thinking that the little things don't count any more, just because you know each other fairly well. Phrases like "please," "thank you," "I'm sorry," and "I love you" never go out of fashion, and they serve as the steady rigging that will hold your relationship on course. Uncommon courtesy includes following through on your promises, being on time, remembering birthdays, returning phone calls, listening carefully, and generally treating your loved ones as if they were the most special people in your entire life—which they are!

Learn From Your Experiences

A relationship is full of lessons, and you only learn from relationships' experiences if you make a conscious effort to do so. So many people get caught up in what or who is right or wrong instead of looking at the lesson that can be learned from the relationship.

The key is to take the experiences—those everyday occurrences in a relationship—and use them to change and grow. That's what a relationship is all about really—change. The only real constant in a relationship is that circumstances and people change. Inspired by experience, change is all around.

We would rather avoid the painful relationship experiences. Losing a loved one, enduring divorce, or falling ill can all be unpleasant and painful, but if we look for the lesson and use the experience to guide us, we can come through with a knowledge that far surpasses the academic lessons we learn in school. The experience of getting burned by a hot stove teaches a child to be cautious. Just as the experience of becoming ill can teach us to appreciate our health. Experience can teach us love, patience, appreciation, and gratitude. It can teach us to take better care of ourselves or to be kind. "Experience, is indeed the best teacher."

Moving Forward

For you and your partner or you alone to move forward in achieving your goals and dreams requires self-discipline. An integral part of reaching your goal(s) is to develop a system that fits your style of doing things and allows you to work with progression without being distracted by everyday activities.

Exercise 10-1:

Together or alone in a quiet place, think about your unique characteristics and what your purpose in life is.

Alone or in a relationship, we all have dreams of what we'd like to do, where we'd like to go, and so on. Make a dream list. Write down five important things that would be fun and bring you or the relationship joy.

1.

2.

3.

4.

5.

Write down some action you or the two of you can take to realize some of these dreams.

1.

2.

3.

4.

5.

Write about what you think is your purpose in life, individually, or the purpose of the relationship.

Based on your purpose in life and the values you hold, write a mission statement for yourself or your relationship.

Now, write five steps you can take to accomplish your, or the relationship's, mission.

1.

2.

3.

4.

5.

Part 11:

Appendix

PART ELEVEN: APPENDIX

Epilogue

Congratulations. You have now finished *Personal Relationships: The Art of Living Together*. Hopefully you have discovered important insights about yourself, and your partner, and have made an honest effort to complete the exercises contained in this book.

You've probably also learned new ways to discuss the similarities and differences you share with your partner and loved ones. These are valuable tools as you assess the strengths in your relationships and consider various ways in which you would like to grow. No doubt there are things you would like to work on in yourself and other issues that will require mutual effort. Perhaps you feel your commitment is greatly renewed. Or maybe you have discovered areas of concern that require further contemplation.

The fascinating thing about a relationship is that it's never static. It transforms from one moment to the next, depending on the moods, maturity, and life circumstances of each of the partners. So do not consider the results of your SAS assessments to be cast in concrete. You can change, and your partner can change—particularly if you both value the relationship and are willing to make emotional investments in your future together.

If you want your relationship to last, you can take no better action than to review this book and re-do its exercises once a year. You'll find that both you and your partner will have made significant progress, in ways that you may not have discussed or explained to each other. By re-articulating who you are, and practicing communication techniques on a regular basis, you will add fresh dimensions to your relationship and build in opportunities for creating depth and understanding. After all, that's what we all really want—someone who genuinely knows us, loves us for who we are, and is capable of receiving equally ample love in return.

So enjoy your relationship together and all of the unique facets you are discovering in each other. I look forward to meeting you again at the beginning of the book next year!

Marti Eicholz, 1998
Kirkland, Washington

Further Journeys

Much of the author's professional life has been devoted to researching human behavior, as well as to studying, testing, and applying various self-awareness tools. Strategies, materials, and modules are continually being developed that you can use every day. Your ideas and comments are of particular interest. To request more information please contact:

Institute for Transformation
550 Kirkland Way, Suite 405
Kirkland, WA 98033
Telephone: 425-739-6025
Fax: 425-739-0022
Toll-free: 1-888-942-9777
E-mail: institute@transformation.org
World Wide Web site: http://www.transformation.org

Please contact the Institute for Transformation for information on other programs offered:

- Seminars and workshops
- Audio tape series on *The Gift of Self-Awareness*
- On-Line Professional Training Programs

  ▲ *Diversity and Cross-Cultural Awareness—Maximizing Human Communications*
  ▲ *Behavior: Keys to Understanding—Maximizing Human Potential*
  ▲ *The Quest for Personal Selling: Transforming Your Communication Style*

Contact www.mecaprofiles.org for information on:

- *MECA Management Programs*™
- Software Programs—PRO SCAN, JOB SCAN, TEAM SCAN

Books and publications available:

- *Personal Development Through Self-Awareness* by Marti Eicholz
- *Inner You/Outer You: Your Guide to Self Discovery* by Marti Eicholz
- *Inspirations for Everyday Life: The Powerful Potential of the Real You* by Marti Eicholz
- *Research in Behavior*
- *Understanding Emotion and Behavior Adjustments*
- *Understanding Stress and Behavior Adjustments*
- *Understanding Energy and Behavior Adjustments*
- *Understanding Self-Esteem and Behavior Adjustments*

Coming soon:

- *Opening Doors to Revitalize Your Relationships*

Additional Reading

In your journey of learning how to develop and maintain healthy, fulfilling personal relationships, you may want to read some of the following books:

Bradshaw on: The Family, John Bradshaw. Health Communications, Inc., Deerfield Beach, FL, 1988. A revolutionary approach to relationships and self-discovery.

Communication Miracles for Couples, Jonathan Robinson. Canari Press, Berkley, CA, 1997. Easy and effective tools to create more love and less conflict in relationships.

Creating Love, John Bradshaw. Bantam Books, New York, NY, 1982. A philosophical presentation of the next great stage of personal growth.

Family Ties That Bind, Dr. Ronald W. Richardson. Int. SelfPress Ltd., 1987. A guide to personal change through understanding family-of-origin issues.

I Will Never Leave You, Hugh and Gayle Prather. Bantam Books, New York, NY, 1995. A presentation of how couples can achieve the power of lasting love.

Love's Journey, Michael Gurian. Shambhala Publications, Inc., Boston, MA, 1995. The seasons and stages of relationships.

Love Lessons, Dr. Brenda Wads and Brenda L. Richardson. Amistad Publishing, New York, NY, 1993. A guide to transforming relationships.

Men Are From Mars, Women Are From Venus, John Gray, Ph.D. HarperCollins Publishing, New York, NY, 1992. A practical guide for improving communication and getting what you want in your relationships.

Men, Women, and Relationships, John Gray, Ph.D. HarperCollins Publishing, New York, NY, 1996. The roles men and women play in relationships and keys to successful interactions.

Straight Talk, Sherod Miller, Ph.D., Daniel Wackman, Ph.D., Elam Nunnally, Ph.D., and Carol Saline. Penguin Books, New York, NY, 1982. A new approach to getting closer to others by saying what you really mean.

The 8 Essential Traits of Couples Who Thrive, Susan Page. Bantam Doubleday Dell Publishing Group, Inc., New York, NY 1994. Pointers to live and love like honeymooners—no matter how long you've been married.

The Road Less Traveled, M. Scott Peck, M.D. A Touchstone Book, Simon & Schuster, New York, NY, 1978. A new psychology of love, traditional values, and spiritual growth.

The 7 Habits of Highly Effective People, Stephen R. Covey. A Fireside Book, Simon & Schuster, New York, NY, 1990. A holistic, integrated, and principle-centered approach to solving personal and professional problems.

Understanding How Others Misunderstand You, Ken Voges and Ron Braund. Moody Press, Chicago, IL, 1995. A unique and proven plan for strengthening personal relationships.

Unlimited Power, Anthony Robbins. Ballatine Books, New York, NY, 1986. A guide to peak personal achievement—it's not about power over other people, it's about power over yourself.

Additional Survey and Request Forms

The Appendix contains copies of the Self-Awareness Survey (SAS) forms. These extra forms are for giving to others to see how they view you and for your use in the future.

Your Self-Awareness Survey

1. Select the word group that best describes you:

D1	D2	D3	D4
· placid · subservient · lacking in self-confidence · yielding · submissive · fearful · easily taken advantage of · never assertive · extremely gentle	· meek · genuine · dependent · hesitant · deferring · submitting · apprehensive · selfless · rarely assertive · very gentle	· mild · gentle · peace-loving · modest · composed · sometimes assertive · congenial · willing · humble · soft · yielding	· certain · curious · discreet · supportive · sometimes leader · sometimes follower · adaptable in groups · relatively assertive

D5	D6	D7	Write selection:
			(For example, D2)
· firm · competitive · decisive · confident · self-assured · definite · positive · happy as leader · usually assertive	· forceful · aspiring · authoritative · bold · direct · adventuresome · keen · analytical · the leader, or nothing	· cynical · brazen · superior · aggressive · commanding · fearless · daring · sharp · coura-geous · always assertive · criticized for cruelty	

2. Select the word group that best describes you:

E1	E2	E3	E4
· withdrawn · secretive · socially selective · aloof · solitary · loner · skeptical · crowd-hater · lost in inner world	· individualistic · shy · serious · introspective · pensive · confidential · timid · guarded · uncomfortable in crowds · happy in solitude	· contemplative · reserved · quiet · private · creative · imaginative · selective · communicative · enjoyer of inner-world · thought-ful	· poised · neighborly · sincere · earnest · genial · friendly · sometimes alone · sometimes social · flexible with others · comfortable as both star and wallflower

E5	E6	E7	Write selection:
			(For example, E4)
· fun-loving · enthusias-tic · friendly · humor-ous · cordial · optimis-tic · good-natured · convincing · group-oriented · often center of attention	· eager · light-hearted · joyful · hospitable · fluent · trusting · excit-ing · decisive · innova-tive · rarely alone · almost always in group · usually center of attention	· promoting · talkative · gregarious · zealous · effusive· demonstrative · lavish · eloquent · never alone · always center of attention · very public person	

3. Select the word group that best describes you:

P1	P2	P3	P4
· brusque · impetuous · coiled spring · sporadic · intense · short-focused · volatile · out of control of emotions · always impulsive	· quick-witted · swift · innovative · driving · hasty · abrupt · reactive · impatient · urgent · often impulsive · prioritizer of own agenda	· active · quick · fast-paced · restless · initiator · action-oriented · pusher · pace-setter · on occasion impulsive	· easy-going · adaptable · adjustable · responsive · sometimes long fuse · sometimes short fuse · balanced agenda with others

P5	P6	P7	Write selection:
· patient · dependable · accommodating · steady · thoughtful · amiable · mild · non-judgmental · non-demonstrative · occasionally angry	· compassionate · cooperative · consistent · kind · sensitive · warm · persistent · emotion avoider · altruistic · rarely angry	· stoic · selfless · hider of emotions · unhurried · passive · hesitant · tolerant · sympathetic · complacent · saint-like patience · never angry · indifferent	*(For example, P4)*

4. Select the word group that best describes you:

S1	S2	S3	S4
· antagonistic · hostile · disagreeable · resistant · defiant · self-governing · disobedient · rebellious · anti-establishment · iconoclast	· disliker of authority · resentful of orders · free-thinker · adventur-ous · contrary · disavower of rules · very independent · visionary	· multi-faceted · "big picture" type · unstruc-tured · uninhibited · broad-minded · rational-izer · not fond of details	· supportive · orderly · open-minded · curious · sometimes compliant · sometimes rule breaker · adaptable · obstreperous · tolerant of many perspectives

S5	S6	S7	Write selection:
· procedural · faithful · systems-oriented · detailer · dutiful · steadfast · committed · careful · fussy about details · relatively obedient · well-orga-nized · enjoyer of structure	· disciplined · methodi-cal · highly obedient · conscientious · devoted · concerned · cautious · fond of details · often fearful · perfectionistic	· subservient · live by the book · exacting · meticulous · dependent · stickler for *all* rules · over-preparer · super-perfectionist · some-times paralyzed by fear	*(For example, S4)*

5. To determine how much energy you have to accomplish tasks, select the word **G** group that best describes your present state. It is important to note that your response may vary according to your present life's circumstances at this time. For the purposes of determining your present energy level, select how you have felt most frequently during the past month or two:

G1	G2	G3	G4
· accident-prone · often sick · a substance abuser · lethargic · seriously depressed · suicidal · surrounded by life crises	· easily fatigued · unfocused · difficulty completing projects · overwhelmed · inactive · illness prone	· sufficient energy · sometimes ill · limited exercise · average productivity · easily diverted	· moderate energy · productive even with diversions · average health · normal fitness · sense of well-being

G5	G6	G7	Write selection:
			(For example, G4)
· plenty of energy · strong · healthy · rarely exhausted · enjoyer of exercise · productive all day · resilient	· endless energy · competent to handle myriad projects at once · hard driver · in need of lots of stimulus · frequent exerciser	· extraordinary energy · overpowering · tireless · dynamo · never ill · never still · constantly restless	

Your Self-Awareness Graph

Name: _____ Date: _____

	D	E	P	S	G
7					
6					
5					
4					
3					
2					
1					

D = Dominance   E = Extroversion   P = Patience   S = Structure   G = Energy Level

Sample Graph

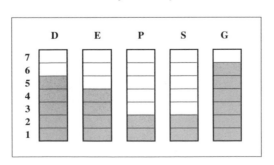

Your Self-Awareness Survey

1. Select the word group that best describes you:

D1	D2	D3	D4
· placid · subservient · lacking in self-confidence · yielding · submissive · fearful · easily taken advantage of · never assertive · extremely gentle	· meek · genuine · dependent · hesitant · deferring · submitting · apprehensive · selfless · rarely assertive · very gentle	· mild · gentle · peace-loving · modest · composed · sometimes assertive · congenial · willing · humble · soft · yielding	· certain · curious · discreet · supportive · sometimes leader · sometimes follower · adaptable in groups · relatively assertive

D5	D6	D7	Write selection:
			(For example, D2)
· firm · competitive · decisive · confident · self-assured · definite · positive · happy as leader · usually assertive	· forceful · aspiring · authoritative · bold · direct · adventuresome · keen · analytical · the leader, or nothing	· cynical · brazen · superior · aggressive · commanding · fearless · daring · sharp · courageous · always assertive · criticized for cruelty	

2. Select the word group that best describes you:

E1	E2	E3	E4
· withdrawn · secretive · socially selective · aloof · solitary · loner · skeptical · crowd-hater · lost in inner world	· individualistic · shy · serious · introspective · pensive · confidential · timid · guarded · uncomfortable in crowds · happy in solitude	· contemplative · reserved · quiet · private · creative · imaginative · selective · communicative · enjoyer of inner-world · thoughtful	· poised · neighborly · sincere · earnest · genial · friendly · sometimes alone · sometimes social · flexible with others · comfortable as both star and wallflower

E5	E6	E7	Write selection:
			(For example, E4)
· fun-loving · enthusiastic · friendly · humorous · cordial · optimistic · good-natured · convincing · group-oriented · often center of attention	· eager · light-hearted · joyful · hospitable · fluent · trusting · exciting · decisive · innovative · rarely alone · almost always in group · usually center of attention	· promoting · talkative · gregarious · zealous · effusive· demonstrative · lavish · eloquent · never alone · always center of attention · very public person	

3. Select the word group that best describes you:

P1	P2	P3	P4
· brusque · impetuous · coiled spring · sporadic · intense · short-focused · volatile · out of control of emotions · always impulsive	· quick-witted · swift · innovative · driving · hasty · abrupt · reactive · impatient · urgent · often impulsive · prioritizer of own agenda	· active · quick · fast-paced · restless · initiator · action-oriented · pusher · pace-setter · on occasion impulsive	· easy-going · adaptable · adjustable · responsive · sometimes long fuse · sometimes short fuse · balanced agenda with others

P5	P6	P7	Write selection:
· patient · dependable · accommodating · steady · thoughtful · amiable · mild · non-judgmental · non-demonstrative · occasionally angry	· compassionate · cooperative · consistent · kind · sensitive · warm · persistent · emotion avoider · altruistic · rarely angry	· stoic · selfless · hider of emotions · unhurried · passive · hesitant · tolerant · sympathetic · complacent · saint-like patience · never angry · indifferent	*(For example, P4)*

4. Select the word group that best describes you:

S1	S2	S3	S4
· antagonistic · hostile · disagreeable · resistant · defiant · self-governing · disobedient · rebellious · anti-establishment · iconoclast	· disliker of authority · resentful of orders · free-thinker · adventur-ous · contrary · disavower of rules · very independent · visionary	· multi-faceted · "big picture" type · unstruc-tured · uninhibited · broad-minded · rational-izer · not fond of details	· supportive · orderly · open-minded · curious · sometimes compliant · sometimes rule breaker · adaptable · obstreperous · tolerant of many perspectives

S5	S6	S7	Write selection:
· procedural · faithful · systems-oriented · detailer · dutiful · steadfast · committed · careful · fussy about details · relatively obedient · well-orga-nized · enjoyer of structure	· disciplined · methodi-cal · highly obedient · conscientious · devoted · concerned · cautious · fond of details · often fearful · perfectionistic	· subservient · live by the book · exacting · meticulous · dependent · stickler for *all* rules · over-preparer · super-perfectionist · some-times paralyzed by fear	*(For example, S4)*

5. To determine how much energy you have to accomplish tasks, select the word **G** group that best describes your present state. It is important to note that your response may vary according to your present life's circumstances at this time. For the purposes of determining your present energy level, select how you have felt most frequently during the past month or two:

G1	G2	G3	G4
· accident-prone · often sick · a substance abuser · lethargic · seriously depressed · suicidal · surrounded by life crises	· easily fatigued · unfocused · difficulty completing projects · overwhelmed · inactive · illness prone	· sufficient energy · sometimes ill · limited exercise · average productivity · easily diverted	· moderate energy · productive even with diversions · average health · normal fitness · sense of well-being

G5	G6	G7	Write selection:
			(For example, G4)
· plenty of energy · strong · healthy · rarely exhausted · enjoyer of exercise · productive all day · resilient	· endless energy · competent to handle myriad projects at once · hard driver · in need of lots of stimulus · frequent exerciser	· extraordinary energy · overpowering · tireless · dynamo · never ill · never still · constantly restless	

Your Self-Awareness Graph

Name: _____   Date: _____

	D	**E**	**P**	**S**	**G**

7
6
5
4
3
2
1

D = Dominance   E = Extroversion   P = Patience   S = Structure   G = Energy Level

Sample Graph

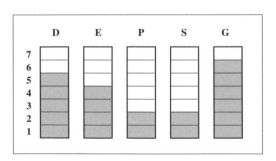

Your Self-Awareness Survey

1. Select the word group that best describes you:

D1	D2	D3	D4
· placid · subservient · lacking in self-confidence · yielding · submissive · fearful · easily taken advantage of · never assertive · extremely gentle	· meek · genuine · dependent · hesitant · deferring · submitting · apprehensive · selfless · rarely assertive · very gentle	· mild · gentle · peace-loving · modest · composed · sometimes assertive · congenial · willing · humble · soft · yielding	· certain · curious · discreet · supportive · sometimes leader · sometimes follower · adaptable in groups · relatively assertive

D5	D6	D7	Write selection:
			(For example, D2)
· firm · competitive · decisive · confident · self-assured · definite · positive · happy as leader · usually assertive	· forceful · aspiring · authoritative · bold · direct · adventuresome · keen · analytical · the leader, or nothing	· cynical · brazen · superior · aggressive · commanding · fearless · daring · sharp · coura-geous · always assertive · criticized for cruelty	

2. Select the word group that best describes you:

E1	E2	E3	E4
· withdrawn · secretive · socially selective · aloof · solitary · loner · skeptical · crowd-hater · lost in inner world	· individualistic · shy · serious · introspective · pensive · confidential · timid · guarded · uncomfortable in crowds · happy in solitude	· contemplative · reserved · quiet · private · creative · imaginative · selective · communicative · enjoyer of inner-world · thought-ful	· poised · neighborly · sincere · earnest · genial · friendly · sometimes alone · sometimes social · flexible with others · comfortable as both star and wallflower

E5	E6	E7	Write selection:
			(For example, E4)
· fun-loving · enthusias-tic · friendly · humor-ous · cordial · optimis-tic · good-natured · convincing · group-oriented · often center of attention	· eager · light-hearted · joyful · hospitable · fluent · trusting · excit-ing · decisive · innova-tive · rarely alone · almost always in group · usually center of attention	· promoting · talkative · gregarious · zealous · effusive· demonstrative · lavish · eloquent · never alone · always center of attention · very public person	

3. Select the word group that best describes you:

P1	P2	P3	P4
· brusque · impetuous · coiled spring · sporadic · intense · short-focused · volatile · out of control of emotions · always impulsive	· quick-witted · swift · innovative · driving · hasty · abrupt · reactive · impatient · urgent · often impulsive · prioritizer of own agenda	· active · quick · fast-paced · restless · initiator · action-oriented · pusher · pace-setter · on occasion impulsive	· easy-going · adaptable · adjustable · responsive · sometimes long fuse · sometimes short fuse · balanced agenda with others

P5	P6	P7	Write selection:
			(For example, P4)
· patient · dependable · accommodating · steady · thoughtful · amiable · mild · non-judgmental · non-demonstrative · occasionally angry	· compassionate · cooperative · consistent · kind · sensitive · warm · persistent · emotion avoider · altruistic · rarely angry	· stoic · selfless · hider of emotions · unhurried · passive · hesitant · tolerant · sympathetic · complacent · saint-like patience · never angry · indifferent	

4. Select the word group that best describes you:

S1	S2	S3	S4
· antagonistic · hostile · disagreeable · resistant · defiant · self-governing · disobedient · rebellious · anti-establishment · iconoclast	· disliker of authority · resentful of orders · free-thinker · adventurous · contrary · disavower of rules · very independent · visionary	· multi-faceted · "big picture" type · unstructured · uninhibited · broad-minded · rationalizer · not fond of details	· supportive · orderly · open-minded · curious · sometimes compliant · sometimes rule breaker · adaptable · obstreperous · tolerant of many perspectives

S5	S6	S7	Write selection:
			(For example, S4)
· procedural · faithful · systems-oriented · detailer · dutiful · steadfast · committed · careful · fussy about details · relatively obedient · well-organized · enjoyer of structure	· disciplined · methodical · highly obedient · conscientious · devoted · concerned · cautious · fond of details · often fearful · perfectionistic	· subservient · live by the book · exacting · meticulous · dependent · stickler for *all* rules · over-preparer · super-perfectionist · sometimes paralyzed by fear	

5.   To determine how much energy you have to accomplish tasks, select the word **G** group that best describes your present state. It is important to note that your response may vary according to your present life's circumstances at this time. For the purposes of determining your present energy level, select how you have felt most frequently during the past month or two:

G1	G2	G3	G4
· accident-prone · often sick · a substance abuser · lethargic · seriously depressed · suicidal · surrounded by life crises	· easily fatigued · unfocused · difficulty completing projects · overwhelmed · inactive · illness prone	· sufficient energy · sometimes ill · limited exercise · average productivity · easily diverted	· moderate energy · productive even with diversions · average health · normal fitness · sense of well-being

G5	G6	G7	Write selection:
			(For example, G4)
· plenty of energy · strong · healthy · rarely exhausted · enjoyer of exercise · productive all day · resilient	· endless energy · competent to handle myriad projects at once · hard driver · in need of lots of stimulus · frequent exerciser	· extraordinary energy · overpowering · tireless · dynamo · never ill · never still · constantly restless	

Your Self-Awareness Graph

Name: _____   Date: _____

	D	**E**	**P**	**S**	**G**

D = Dominance   E = Extroversion   P = Patience   S = Structure   G = Energy Level

Sample Graph

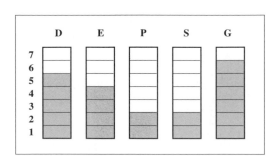

Your Self-Awareness Survey

1. Select the word group that best describes you:

D1	D2	D3	D4
· placid · subservient · lacking in self-confidence · yielding · submissive · fearful · easily taken advantage of · never assertive · extremely gentle	· meek · genuine · dependent · hesitant · deferring · submitting · apprehensive · selfless · rarely assertive · very gentle	· mild · gentle · peace-loving · modest · composed · sometimes assertive · congenial · willing · humble · soft · yielding	· certain · curious · discreet · supportive · sometimes leader · sometimes follower · adaptable in groups · relatively assertive

D5	D6	D7	Write selection:
· firm · competitive · decisive · confident · self-assured · definite · positive · happy as leader · usually assertive	· forceful · aspiring · authoritative · bold · direct · adventuresome · keen · analytical · the leader, or nothing	· cynical · brazen · superior · aggressive · commanding · fearless · daring · sharp · coura-geous · always assertive · criticized for cruelty	*(For example, D2)*

2. Select the word group that best describes you:

E1	E2	E3	E4
· withdrawn · secretive · socially selective · aloof · solitary · loner · skeptical · crowd-hater · lost in inner world	· individualistic · shy · serious · introspective · pensive · confidential · timid · guarded · uncomfortable in crowds · happy in solitude	· contemplative · reserved · quiet · private · creative · imaginative · selective · communicative · enjoyer of inner-world · thought-ful	· poised · neighborly · sincere · earnest · genial · friendly · sometimes alone · sometimes social · flexible with others · comfortable as both star and wallflower

E5	E6	E7	Write selection:
· fun-loving · enthusias-tic · friendly · humor-ous · cordial · optimis-tic · good-natured · convincing · group-oriented · often center of attention	· eager · light-hearted · joyful · hospitable · fluent · trusting · excit-ing · decisive · innova-tive · rarely alone · almost always in group · usually center of attention	· promoting · talkative · gregarious · zealous · effusive· demonstrative · lavish · eloquent · never alone · always center of attention · very public person	*(For example, E4)*

3. Select the word group that best describes you:

P1	P2	P3	P4
· brusque · impetuous · coiled spring · sporadic · intense · short-focused · volatile · out of control of emotions · always impulsive	· quick-witted · swift · innovative · driving · hasty · abrupt · reactive · impatient · urgent · often impulsive · prioritizer of own agenda	· active · quick · fast-paced · restless · initiator · action-oriented · pusher · pace-setter · on occasion impulsive	· easy-going · adaptable · adjustable · responsive · sometimes long fuse · sometimes short fuse · balanced agenda with others

P5	P6	P7	Write selection:
· patient · dependable · accommodating · steady · thoughtful · amiable · mild · non-judgmental · non-demonstrative · occasionally angry	· compassionate · cooperative · consistent · kind · sensitive · warm · persistent · emotion avoider · altruistic · rarely angry	· stoic · selfless · hider of emotions · unhurried · passive · hesitant · tolerant · sympathetic · complacent · saint-like patience · never angry · indifferent	*(For example, P4)*

4. Select the word group that best describes you:

S1	S2	S3	S4
· antagonistic · hostile · disagreeable · resistant · defiant · self-governing · disobedient · rebellious · anti-establishment · iconoclast	· disliker of authority · resentful of orders · free-thinker · adventur-ous · contrary · disavower of rules · very independent · visionary	· multi-faceted · "big picture" type · unstruc-tured · uninhibited · broad-minded · rational-izer · not fond of details	· supportive · orderly · open-minded · curious · sometimes compliant · sometimes rule breaker · adaptable · obstreperous · tolerant of many perspectives

S5	S6	S7	Write selection:
· procedural · faithful · systems-oriented · detailer · dutiful · steadfast · committed · careful · fussy about details · relatively obedient · well-orga-nized · enjoyer of structure	· disciplined · methodi-cal · highly obedient · conscientious · devoted · concerned · cautious · fond of details · often fearful · perfectionistic	· subservient · live by the book · exacting · meticulous · dependent · stickler for *all* rules · over-preparer · super-perfectionist · some-times paralyzed by fear	*(For example, S4)*

5. To determine how much energy you have to accomplish tasks, select the word **G** group that best describes your present state. It is important to note that your response may vary according to your present life's circumstances at this time. For the purposes of determining your present energy level, select how you have felt most frequently during the past month or two:

G1	G2	G3	G4
· accident-prone · often sick · a substance abuser · lethargic · seriously depressed · suicidal · surrounded by life crises	· easily fatigued · unfocused · difficulty completing projects · overwhelmed · inactive · illness prone	· sufficient energy · sometimes ill · limited exercise · average productivity · easily diverted	· moderate energy · productive even with diversions · average health · normal fitness · sense of well-being

G5	G6	G7	Write selection:
			(For example, G4)
· plenty of energy · strong · healthy · rarely exhausted · enjoyer of exercise · productive all day · resilient	· endless energy · competent to handle myriad projects at once · hard driver · in need of lots of stimulus · frequent exerciser	· extraordinary energy · overpowering · tireless · dynamo · never ill · never still · constantly restless	

Your Self-Awareness Graph

Name: _____   Date: _____

	D	**E**	**P**	**S**	**G**
7					
6					
5					
4					
3					
2					
1					

D = Dominance   E = Extroversion   P = Patience   S = Structure   G = Energy Level

Sample Graph

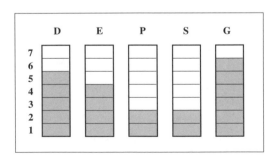

Your Self-Awareness Survey

1. Select the word group that best describes you:

D1	D2	D3	D4
· placid · subservient · lacking in self-confidence · yielding · submissive · fearful · easily taken advantage of · never assertive · extremely gentle	· meek · genuine · dependent · hesitant · deferring · submitting · apprehensive · selfless · rarely assertive · very gentle	· mild · gentle · peace-loving · modest · composed · sometimes assertive · congenial · willing · humble · soft · yielding	· certain · curious · discreet · supportive · sometimes leader · sometimes follower · adaptable in groups · relatively assertive

D5	D6	D7	Write selection:
			(For example, D2)
· firm · competitive · decisive · confident · self-assured · definite · positive · happy as leader · usually assertive	· forceful · aspiring · authoritative · bold · direct · adventuresome · keen · analytical · the leader, or nothing	· cynical · brazen · superior · aggressive · commanding · fearless · daring · sharp · coura-geous · always assertive · criticized for cruelty	

2. Select the word group that best describes you:

E1	E2	E3	E4
· withdrawn · secretive · socially selective · aloof · solitary · loner · skeptical · crowd-hater · lost in inner world	· individualistic · shy · serious · introspective · pensive · confidential · timid · guarded · uncomfortable in crowds · happy in solitude	· contemplative · reserved · quiet · private · creative · imaginative · selective · communicative · enjoyer of inner-world · thought-ful	· poised · neighborly · sincere · earnest · genial · friendly · sometimes alone · sometimes social · flexible with others · comfortable as both star and wallflower

E5	E6	E7	Write selection:
			(For example, E4)
· fun-loving · enthusias-tic · friendly · humor-ous · cordial · optimis-tic · good-natured · convincing · group-oriented · often center of attention	· eager · light-hearted · joyful · hospitable · fluent · trusting · excit-ing · decisive · innova-tive · rarely alone · almost always in group · usually center of attention	· promoting · talkative · gregarious · zealous · effusive· demonstrative · lavish · eloquent · never alone · always center of attention · very public person	

3. Select the word group that best describes you:

P1	P2	P3	P4
· brusque · impetuous · coiled spring · sporadic · intense · short-focused · volatile · out of control of emotions · always impulsive	· quick-witted · swift · innovative · driving · hasty · abrupt · reactive · impatient · urgent · often impulsive · prioritizer of own agenda	· active · quick · fast-paced · restless · initiator · action-oriented · pusher · pace-setter · on occasion impulsive	· easy-going · adaptable · adjustable · responsive · sometimes long fuse · sometimes short fuse · balanced agenda with others

P5	P6	P7	Write selection:
			(For example, P4)
· patient · dependable · accommodating · steady · thoughtful · amiable · mild · non-judgmental · non-demonstrative · occasionally angry	· compassionate · cooperative · consistent · kind · sensitive · warm · persistent · emotion avoider · altruistic · rarely angry	· stoic · selfless · hider of emotions · unhurried · passive · hesitant · tolerant · sympathetic · complacent · saint-like patience · never angry · indifferent	

4. Select the word group that best describes you:

S1	S2	S3	S4
· antagonistic · hostile · disagreeable · resistant · defiant · self-governing · disobedient · rebellious · anti-establishment · iconoclast	· disliker of authority · resentful of orders · free-thinker · adventur-ous · contrary · disavower of rules · very independent · visionary	· multi-faceted · "big picture" type · unstruc-tured · uninhibited · broad-minded · rational-izer · not fond of details	· supportive · orderly · open-minded · curious · sometimes compliant · sometimes rule breaker · adaptable · obstreperous · tolerant of many perspectives

S5	S6	S7	Write selection:
			(For example, S4)
· procedural · faithful · systems-oriented · detailer · dutiful · steadfast · committed · careful · fussy about details · relatively obedient · well-orga-nized · enjoyer of structure	· disciplined · methodi-cal · highly obedient · conscientious · devoted · concerned · cautious · fond of details · often fearful · perfectionistic	· subservient · live by the book · exacting · meticulous · dependent · stickler for *all* rules · over-preparer · super-perfectionist · some-times paralyzed by fear	

5. To determine how much energy you have to accomplish tasks, select the word **G** group that best describes your present state. It is important to note that your response may vary according to your present life's circumstances at this time. For the purposes of determining your present energy level, select how you have felt most frequently during the past month or two:

G1	G2	G3	G4
· accident-prone · often sick · a substance abuser · lethargic · seriously depressed · suicidal · surrounded by life crises	· easily fatigued · unfocused · difficulty completing projects · overwhelmed · inactive · illness prone	· sufficient energy · sometimes ill · limited exercise · average productivity · easily diverted	· moderate energy · productive even with diversions · average health · normal fitness · sense of well-being

G5	G6	G7	Write selection:
			(For example, G4)
· plenty of energy · strong · healthy · rarely exhausted · enjoyer of exercise · productive all day · resilient	· endless energy · competent to handle myriad projects at once · hard driver · in need of lots of stimulus · frequent exerciser	· extraordinary energy · overpowering · tireless · dynamo · never ill · never still · constantly restless	

Your Self-Awareness Graph

Name: _____   Date: _____

	D	E	P	S	G
7					
6					
5					
4					
3					
2					
1					

D = Dominance   E = Extroversion   P = Patience   S = Structure   G = Energy Level

Sample Graph

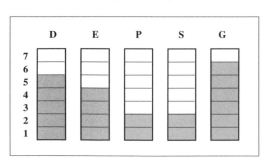

About the Author

Marti Eicholz, Ph.D., is the author of six popular books, including five on behavioral assessment and personal growth and one inspirational guide. She is president and CEO of MECA Profiles Unlimited, Inc., a consulting firm specializing in behavioral assessment, management practices, organizational efficiencies, and morale enhancement for which she was distinguished as an Honored Professional in *Who's Who of Executives and Business Leaders*. Dr. Eicholz is also founder and president of the Institute for Transformation, an educational center devoted to unlocking personal and business potential, in Kirkland, Washington. Known for her dynamic presence and enthusiastic presentations, Dr. Eicholz is currently broadcasting a weekly radio show on *The Gift of Self-Awareness*. She has been an instructor at St. Francis College, Purdue University, Indiana University, and Seattle Pacific University, and is a frequent speaker to national and international audiences.

My Notes

My Notes

My Notes

My Notes

My Notes